Preacher's Son

By
Dewi Williams

This book is dedicated to Luke.

My thanks to all who have helped in the creation of this book and especially to Mrs Ruth Bidgood, Mrs H.George, David and Linda Jones, Mrs O Jones, Alan Marshfield, Bryan and Margaret Watkins, Mr L.M. Williams .... and Hilary Kendrick.

British Library Cataloguing In Publication Data
A Record of this Publication is available
from the British Library

ISBN 1846851866
978-1-84685-186-5

Published 2006 by

Exposure Publishing,
an imprint of Diggory Press,
Three Rivers, Minions, Liskeard, Cornwall,
PL14 5LE, UK
WWW.DIGGORYPRESS.COM

Chapters

Chapter One
First Impressions

Approximately ten miles north by north west of Swansea lies the little hamlet of Hendy as close as a stone's throw to its bigger brother of Pontardulais. This is where I first saw the light of day, or perhaps to be a little more precise, I first saw the dark of night as I am led to believe that I was born at 3.45. in the morning on the 27th of November 1942. It was probably very dark, rather wet, cold and because of the British government's little altercation with Herr Hitler and his frenzied followers, in a blackout!

Pontardulais, a bridge over the river of two voices, is in Glamorganshire whilst Hendy is in Carmarthenshire and although I have no inkling as to the exact location of the border I can vouchsafe that I was born on the right, or is it the wrong, side of the tracks. My passport is inscribed with the word Dyfed which adds to the confusion and led to an American customs officer in Detroit scratching his head in a total state of bewilderment not having the faintest pointer as to the proximity of this Welsh where about.

But to return to November 27th 1942. The war in Europe was well into its stride and the Luftwaffe had practically demolished all that was left of the old part of Swansea with its night time bombing raids but for some reason known only, I suspect, to Goerring and his high flying companions, the bombings ceased between July 1942 and February 1943 which gave my mother a somewhat calmer environment to prepare for my imminent arrival. I have no dubiety in my mind that my mother was a disappointed woman. Having already produced my older brother Gareth in 1940, she had secretly longed for a daughter to be a sister and natural companion to my brother and when I descended on the scene so to speak not I'm afraid, trailing clouds of glory, she was left stunned and quite frankly disconcerted. Had she not told the attending nurse? "Oh not another boy,.....?" This was a phrase I was to hear many times in my infancy and one which haunts and slightly disturbs me to this day. But there may have been other reasons for her contingency. I was born in the bed in which I now sleep. I was born in the house with the doctor and midwife in attendance. My sister Hefina was the only one of we four that had been born in a hospital. There had been another boy.

My mother seldom talked about her first born child. She rarely responded to an infant's natural inquisitiveness and would not be drawn on the question. It became almost a taboo subject within the family and even towards the end of her life the acute sense of sadness was too painful for my mother to talk about her loss and I have merely gained snippets of information snared from one or two close members of the kith and kin. Some things in all families are never discussed for whatever the reason. The death of my brother was such an example. He was born in 1938 and lived for six days. I have in my possession a forlorn and rather creased and crumpled certificate recording the sober and uncompromising cold fact. He is buried in an unmarked spot in a little graveyard near Hendy on the side of a hill in a quiet corner near the gentle green and growing hazel trees. They had christened him Gerallt.

Life at that time was very difficult for the majority of people. Britain had just dragged its feet out of the slough of depression and the snarling threat of an aggressive German army was waiting around every corner. There was no National Health system, wages were very low, my father's pittance as a Parish priest was less than adequate to maintain a growing family and my eldest brother received very little help in his brief and futile struggle for life. Some had said he was born with severe problems; others have muttered the word doctor and let the rest of the unfinished sentence drift away with the wind as they shook their head. My brother too just drifted away.

My father, Alun Rhys Williams, was born in 1910 in a little village near Clydach, Swansea called Craigcefnparc. The village is an assortment of houses and small holdings, a few shops, one or two pubs, a closed colliery, a couple of chapels namely Elim and Pantycrwys, a primary school and a church. My grandfather, Noah Williams was a cobbler or more precisely a shoemaker who practised his trade from a modest but robust detached house on the side of a hill overlooking the little valley. He also had two fields, a cow and a pig. On a clear day from the house one can see Swansea quite clearly and can easily identify the cooling towers of Skewen in the distance. My father was the eldest of seven children, three boys and four girls and his uncle, my grandfather's brother was the Rev. Crwys Williams who became the Arch Druid of the National Eisteddfod and was one of the greatest Welsh lyrical poets publishing several volumes of poetry and stories in his long and celebrated lifetime. In 1948 at the National Eisteddfod, held that year in Mountain Ash, he had the honour of accepting the then Princess Elizabeth into the bardic circle. I have a clip of this moment on video and it is ironic to see the future queen of England bowing to my great uncle as he stands there in full regalia with arms aloft and a straight face with his tongue quite firmly impressed into his cheek! "Croeso i Elisabeth o Windsor" he proclaims "Welcome to Elizabeth of Windsor."

My mother, Lois Lewis, was born a few miles away in another village, on a hill near Pontardawe called Alltwen. She was born in 1912.Interestingly enough; she too was one of seven children although this equation reads four boys and three girls. Her father, my grandfather, was one William Richard Lewis, miner and later shopkeeper. He, despite his rather regal Christian names was as welsh as Prince Llewelyn. He possessed a fine singing voice, was short and stocky, tough as teak and as bald as an egg. My mother could never remember him with hair. He had told the story many times of having started work in the coal mines at a very tender age and telling us that his own father had gone underground at the age of eight, travelling on his father's shoulders. I believed it all when I was a boy marvelling in the romantic image painted by my grandfather and I believe it now too. I am endowed with more hair than he ever had but I have inherited his miner's forearms and perhaps some of his singing voice!

She, too was brought up in a solid substantial detached house with a garden and a pig, and was used to the company of her brothers and sisters. It was without a doubt a very happy home, with a rocking chair, a grandfather clock and a piano. It was a house that reverberated to the sounds of laughter, good humour and song.

Alltwen was the birthplace too of another fine Welsh poet called Gwenallt. David Gwenallt Jones. It was also the birthplace of a famous boxer of the forties: Ronnie James. He was British and British Empire Lightweight champion when he unsuccessfully challenged the American Ike Williams for the world title in 1946. South Wales was and still is, I fancy, full of beguilingly complexed and charming paradoxes of men. Physically tough men who knew a thing or two about how to throw a punch, how to tackle a front row forward a yard from the line, how to look after themselves and who in the next breath would openly shed tears at a funeral and in a quiet moment compose the most eloquent and deceptively beautiful lines of verse with rhymes of pure grace, wonder and dexterity.

I have little recollection of those early years. Certainly there was a very close knit community based around the chapel. My father's chapel which was congregational in denomination. Capel Newydd and all in Welsh. I had no need to speak English because no -one else did. What glimpses of the past I have are fragments, flotsam on the sea of memory. I know I experienced my first feelings of sexual excitement even at the age of four when I saw a girl in her knickers. I still recoil with horror at my first feeling of guilt after having pushed a boy of similar age, Howard Thomas, down the steps of our house leaving him in a tangle of limbs, spinning tricycle wheels and screams. It seemed then a long descent but in the cold light of day it was a mere two small stone steps.

Our house seemed then a huge abode when in fact it was a mid terraced little house with three bedrooms a bathroom and down stairs two rooms one of which served as father's study. There was a scullery and a back door leading to paved area where I played on my tricycle and where a few steps led up to a nice vegetable garden. My father was a good gardener a recreation he enjoyed all his life. At the end of the garden was a wall and on the other side nettles and waste land. Although it served as the manse it had the rather pretentious name of "Kanowna" the origin of which has eluded me. There was a fairly busy road in front of the house which led to Llangennech, onwards to Llanelli and on the other side of the road was a boggy area, the river and a railway line. I can remember sitting up in bed watching the engines chuffing ponderously along the line. There was more than likely a shunting yard there with the river running behind it. The little engines would puff and stutter, clanking and rattling, shuffling and spluttering and grumbling all the while. There was also a bog land area on the other side of the road where I had to be pulled out by my feet by my brother Gareth who had to call my father for assistance. I have brief snatches of memory of my feet sinking slowly into the mud and feeling myself sliding out of control. There was a hot bath where the water turned to brown as soon as I stepped into it and my mother telling stories of a dog called Black Bob who barked in Welsh as I sat in front of the fire wrapped in a towel. The stories by the fire continued even when later on I contracted a dose of pneumonia and the doctor had to be called. I seemed to slip in and out of consciousness as the low nicotine voices murmured darkly in the shadowed kitchen. I was very hot and feverish refusing to swallow some tablets that had been prescribed. Eventually my father tried to trick me by crushing the tablet and mixing it with jam on a piece of bread which I eventually ate and swallowed and I survived.

There was a "jazz band" and a carnival where the local people dressed up in strange home-made costumes and paraded up and down the roads at some festive occasion or Bank Holiday creating their own music playing kazoos, mouth organs and combs with paper. I distinctly remember wearing a red blazer like a Bobby Shafto with gold coloured buttons. There was a park and country lanes with swings and a roundabout and hazel trees. On the village square was an air raid shelter, strange smelling, dark, damp and mysterious that echoed our every word. There was a butcher's shop by the name of Clement and a public urinal which stank and where I and a pal called John Eaves tried to pee over the wall. We were two little performers creating our own private little rainbows. There were names like Morris, Price and Nicholas and one man known as Tom Yr Allt. He was the local milkman and farmed a small holding on the outskirts of the village. He had a flushed complexion, cheeks like two bruised peaches, eyes that danced and sparkled in all weathers and a very loud laugh that filled the room along with a smile that dazzled and pleased at every turn of phrase. Years later after my father's death I would come across a letter from Tom to my father wishing him well for the future and ending with a rather poignant request that he hoped the children would remember him. It was written in 1948 and yes, I still remember him filling our little parlour with the sunshine of his presence and the intoxication of his laughter.

I have very vague memories of school but I know I attended the Infants because there is a group photograph to prove it. I am sitting on the floor in the front row on the left with my fringe over my forehead, a donkey crop I think it was called, dressed completely in home made clothes skilfully sewn and tailored by my mother. I don't look particularly happy even though I think I must have been. On second thoughts nobody looked very happy in the sepia tinged photograph. I know there was a teacher called rather inappropriately Miss Marker who once praised me for my rendition of a bleating lamb. There is something to be said about a Welsh accented crying of a motherless lamb and although my impersonation has not not exactly become my party piece, nor has my door been hammered upon by theatrical agents requesting my services, it was my first taste of creative praise. One day in the nineteen eighties I stood alone on the concreted playground of Ysgol Fach yr Hendy hoping for inspirational flashes of recognition or some rekindled distant long lost memory. Alas! Nothing! But two experiences stay with me to this day: the singing of the old Welsh hymns and in complete contrast the slow and menacing sound of a low flying aircraft in the heat of the night. There is nothing quite so exhilarating, so uplifting to the spirit, so peculiar to the Welsh race, as hearing a chapel full of people, men and women, congregating together to praise the Lord with their singing of the old Welsh hymns. In my native language this celebration is called Cymanfa Ganu and there is nothing quite like it anywhere else in the world. I must have witnessed it early in my infancy and the deep emotional and inspiring experience leaves an indelible mark on ones psyche. To hear and listen to ordinary people, not necessarily trained voices, experiencing the catharsis as the music swells and the melody rises and falls always entering and then re entering the minor key. The names of the compositions are music in themselves: Crug y bar, Llef, Rhosymedre, Blaenwern just to name but a few.

The war ended in 1945. I don't remember it but there is a rare photograph of me in my mother's arms at the celebration to mark VE day. In the photograph there are lines of tables with happy faces laughing and joking. And there are adult faces, an assortment of tired but grateful faces happy to be there and glad to be alive. I don't recall the celebrations, after all I was only three, but in my deep subconscious I hear the sound of bombs falling. It may have been Swansea or perhaps Bristol, but I hear them clearly and I am aware of huddling under the stairs with my mother and brother, black sinister looking gas mask at the ready, waiting for the sound of the siren to signal the all clear. I am especially aware of the long drawn out cry of the fading dying siren sound like some long suffering wounded animal in the darkness of night. Again sometimes now in the very early hours of the morning entrapped in a sweet dream half awake entangled in the web of warmth I hear the low hum of a solitary aeroplane passing peacefully overhead. It produces a peculiar feeling not as strong as an emotion, merely a feeling of deja vu, a feeling that has no identity and does not answer to a name. My memory leads me back to Swansea where I am holding my mother's hand as we walk in the mid morning silence amongst the twisted and broken streets the blackened walls and smashed windows of half standing buildings where the sewers run amongst the smoking debris of waste and crushed concrete.

In the spring of 1948, my father decided to leave the parish to which he had given so much as a young man having been ordained in 1935 and decided to move to North Breconshire in the heart of Mid Wales. Troedrhiwdalar and its sister chapels. My great adventure was about to begin. My dear little sister had just arrived. She came home one day with my mother, wrapped in a white blanket, an amassment of black curls and strikingly beautiful brown eyes. I loved her from the moment I first beheld her and perched her little pink hand in mine. It was a worrying couple of weeks for my parents when my sister suddenly fell gravely ill and was rushed to hospital. I hate to think what my poor mother was enduring as she relived the agonies of a few years earlier. I have hazy recollections of asking my father if I should ask God to bring her home to us. It transpires that I, in my childish and naive innocence, closed my eyes, put my head on the table, covered my face with my hands and asked God to bring her home. My prayers were answered and peace prevailed once more as the crisis passed and my sister regained her strength and returned to us all laughing and gurgling. There was a minor incident where my sister nearly swallowed a coin but I, being the natural hero, rescued her by swiftly immersing my fingers into her mouth and prising the unwanted invader from her open mouth. I basked once again in the glow of admiration and respect. For several years afterwards I was told the same story of how I had saved my only sister's life and how I had acted with great swift thinking....I never once denied any of it!

I have a copy of my father's letter sent to the secretaries of the new chapels accepting their offer. It was hand written in both Welsh and the new language which was about to confront me. English. As I read its contents now it seems old fashioned and quaintly singular that it is almost amusing had it not been for the fact that it was written with the deepest sincerity and utmost candour.

"To the Churches of Troedrhiwdalar, Capel Rhos, Beulah and Olewydd.
Dear Christian friends

I wish to inform you that I accept the unanimous and fervent invitation you have extended to me that I may serve with you as Christian minister. I have taken this decision after much prayer and meditation and I regard the invitation as an added privilege and honour to me in the work of his kingdom....."

Chapter Two
The Promised Land

In the dark shadows of memory flicker the odd image as if illuminated by the sudden spark of a match, the splash of colour as when a kingfisher dives across the shimmering stream. I would like to think that my arrival at my new home was greeted with great proclaim with hundreds of strange people waving and smiling. This was obviously not the resulting situation. I recall the early hours of the morning two young men in long brown coats wreathed in smiles carrying our meagre belongings into a large Pickford's van and laughing when they discovered a toy automatic pistol under my pillow. There were shouts of goodbye, tears and kisses, hugs and scarves akimbo and a pet cat entrapped in a cardboard box secured with string with air holes in the top.

My father must have gone on ahead either by car driven by somebody else or perhaps with the removal van itself but I travelled with my mother carrying my baby sister Hefina in her arms, my brother, sullen and serious blinking behind his glasses and my Auntie Mary. Auntie Mary was my mother's oldest sister and was endowed with the pioneer spirit. She would have crossed the western plains in a covered wagon but our exodus was by train, GWR from Swansea to Garth on what is now called the Mid Wales line and I remember the increasing excitement of travelling by steam train and entering the Sugar Loaf tunnel between Llandovery and Llanwrtyd Wells. Here the musical accompaniment of the train changed abruptly and the compartment was suddenly engulfed in a black blanket and a curious smell of soot and gas. When dawn broke it was light again and the familiar steady dance rhythm had returned. There was nothing but beauty outside. Rolling hills dotted with sheep, silver streams and green trees, daffodils and snowdrops and the occasional bird of prey hovering above. Or so it seemed through the eyes of a child.

Someone must have met us at Garth station. It might have been Uncle Phil who was husband to Auntie Mary. He was one of the few people in our immediate family to own a car. It was a black, long bodied Wolsley. There were a few people at the house to have a good look at the new preacher and his family. I believe that Cemlyn Price of Tyrosser, a neighbouring farm, was one. Cem was a friendly small teenager with a roman nose and a mouth full of crooked teeth eager to help and always with a smile and a laugh. Mr John Williams of Danyrallt Villa was most certainly there, not only as family friend and benefactor but also as a representative of the chapel or more precisely the group of chapels that my father had been entrusted with. There was also a young woman with jet black hair and shining eyes in the vicinity to assist my mother with the baby and household chores. She was Rita Davies who could speak a little Welsh and as I spoke a little less English managed to engage me in conversation with her dazzling smile and dark brooding good looks.

The house seemed colossal compared with my previous home. It was called Glandulais (by the side of the Dulais river) and was semi detached. There is a touch of irony to discover that I had come from the close proximity of one river to another with the same name. There was a small house next door where lived Mr and Mrs Bryn Evans and their young son Alwyn. There was also an older man who might have been Alwyn's grandfather, called James Jones with white hair and wore black boots. The cottage was known locally as TyTwt although later it became rather pretentiously Glandulais Cottage. We had a large garden with two apple trees a front lawn, un-mowed, some buildings which had been either a stable or a barn, or both, a field which later served as a football pitch and a cricket square and around half a dozen beautiful fir trees bearing cones and both red and grey squirrel. There was also an empty wooden garage with a zinc roof, a wash house and a very basic outside toilet which comprised a wooden seat with an oval hole over a bucket. The little river ran directly past the front garden and at the back of the house behind the field the road rose in a hill to Beulah and beyond.

There was no electricity and no running water save for a tap in the scullery which produced a gushing stream of very cold water after a severe arm twisting competition with the reluctant component. There was a front door and a hallway with flagstone floors, a little room to the left which became my father's study and which always smelled of stale tobacco and old books, a kitchen where we spent most of the time over the table or listening to the wireless, a corridor to the parlour or front room which was spacious, damp and very cold. When a fire was lit in there we were allowed in to either play the piano, an old vertical iron framed model with brass candle holders made by Thompson and Shackell, or to sit quietly. I used to use the sofa as a horse and my sister's safety harness became a bridle which tinkled and sang to my clip clop just like the real thing or so I thought. Many a red skinned warrior met his untimely death in that front room when I rode the Pony Express and delivered the mail across the rolling, riding wild-west. The back door opened to a small patio of cobbled stones interspersed with wild weeds and rather reluctantly fenced in, a coalhouse, the barn and the field.

Upstairs were four bedrooms and I was privileged to bags the one in the front in the middle looking out over the little river Dulais. In this sparse but comfortable, uncarpeted, little room, I had a small cast iron single bed, painted green and a small table with one drawer, a smaller table for my candle and an uncurtained sash window through which at night I could count the stars that rose above the Wennallt woods exchange smiles with the moon and trace the outline of my beloved hills that stood as permanent sentinels guarding and protecting me in my innocence.

We settled in quickly as I remember and the period of adjustment was painless and predictable. There were people calling all the time, shyly introducing themselves bringing with them gifts of eggs, vegetables, cold meat and once or twice a gambo of wood for the fire. Mr John Williams was a constant visitor, his solemn earnest bachelor face breaking into smiles as he spoke a fluent Welsh offering his help and guidance to us all. He could never disguise his obvious pleasure in having us at Glandulais. We were all as a family overwhelmed with the generosity of spirit, the sense of prevailing optimism and kindness and that my father was given the respect that was reserved for the clergy in those days. I splashed and paddled in a pool of sentiment and happiness.

Rita Davies's little step brother Tony came to help me unload my toys. The few possessions I had, were quickly scrutinised, closely examined and an unanimous verdict given on each item. "I've got one of those at home." Every article I displayed to him he claimed to have at home but there was no trace of envy or suspicion. I discovered that I was fourteen days older than Tony and he was to become my close childhood friend. And did he have the same as me at home? No. He had considerably less. He did however possess a number of lead soldiers one of whom I decided to retrieve for myself taking him home in my pocket to play with under the kitchen table. I was gently but firmly made to take him back the next day and I remember feeling the faint pang of conscience. The soldier was dutifully returned to his barracks, had not been reported AWOL and no more was said on the matter. I was five years old and not about to begin a life of petty crime. I was the "preacher's son".

Mrs Jones Penrhiwmoch came calling with eggs and sweet delicious, primrose yellow home made butter along with her son David. He was a year and three days older than me and my first recollection of him was my throwing a tennis ball to him. He grinned, rolled his eyes and threw the ball back to me. I caught it cleanly on the bounce and we were chums from that moment on and maintaining our special friendship half a century or so later.

My other immediate pal was Dennis Jones from Tyisaf. He was the youngest of four brothers and was a year younger than me .His three brothers were all much older than he. They smoked, had been in the forces and displayed a motley collection of tattoos. My mother in a rare moment of indiscretion once said quite simply that Dennis had been a mistake. It was many years before I worked out her allusion. He came galloping over the bridge one day in short trousers and jersey, ink black hair down in his eyes carrying a ball and we too became best friends at the drop of a hat.

All this was so new to me. Each day was an exciting revelation. A new environment, a new set of friends, a new climate although we were only in Breconshire about 50 or so miles away from Hendy. People spoke English most of the time and in a matter of weeks I spoke it as fluently as Dai or Tony or Dennis. There were changes of course. Whereas before, a main road with a bus route had passed my home now a tiny road passed the house to a crossroads about two hundred yards away. There was a signpost with arms pointing in four directions and a head which read Breconshire.C. C. We children used to hurl stones at it to try to break the cast iron frame but we never succeeded. It read four and a half miles to Newbridge on Wye, two and half miles to Beulah, two miles to Garth and a similar distance to Capel y Rhos. This was indeed the centre of my universe and I had little need for anywhere else. The crossing, as it was known locally, was a very integral part of the way of life then. Here the bus that took us once a week to Builth Wells, about ten miles away, stopped to pick up its passengers. Here was the natural area for the parting of the ways and a convivial spot for the young people to meet after Chapel on a Sunday night. I used to sit at my window on a late summer's night trying to hear snippets of conversation through their laughter and merriment. The young women of the parish who would suitably and sensibly be turned out in hat and gloves and sometimes seamed stockings would congregate arm in arm in a show of solidarity whilst the young men, uncomfortable in their ill fitting suits and too tight collars would hang around the fringes in twos or threes smoking woodbines and casting admiring side-long glances at the giggling girls. There was much happy horseplay amongst the cacophony and as the shadows lengthened and the discordant shape of the trees became indistinguishable to me the loud voices became softer and muted drifting off into my slumber. Then the serious business of courting would take place and the boys and girls would pair off and away they would meander the male leading and pushing his bicycle followed meekly by the consenting female. I longed to be older, to be accepted into their fraternity and to share the secrets of their adult world. Someone once said to my father, trying perhaps to stir up some gossip and mischief. "Doesn't the noise they make disturb you Mister Williams?" My father reading the situation very clearly replied with a half smile.

"It's when you cannot hear them is the time to be worried."

Behind the house the main road rose up the hill towards the village of Beulah. This was known as Tyrosser pitch. In North Breconshire a steepish hill is known as a pitch. It was narrow and flanked on both sides of the road with high hedges of blackthorn and hazel. As a young child I would ride my tricycle down half the slope thrilling to the exhilaration of the wind in my ears, the deafening sound of the metallic wheels on the tarmacced surface and the pins and needles sensation in my hands. The trike was a battered old heavy iron cast off probably coming from some relation or other on my mother's side of the family and although it had lasted well for its previous owner it did not survive very long in my presence. I tried the same activity with my little sister's tricycle which was more modern and was painted a vivid red but it had a fixed yellow wheel and the spinning pedals coming down the hill was not appropriate to my liking and the novelty wore off very quickly Half way up the pitch on the right hand side of the road was an old oak tree where I once spotted an owl. The oak's branches hung half way across the road blocking out the sunlight in summer and sheltering us from the rain in winter. It became a familiar landmark to mark the half way point up the hill. Behind the house just outside the field was a rough dirt tracked road which led across the distance of about four fields to the farm of Cimlelwyd. I would journey there sometimes when I was either a drifting cowboy looking for cows to punch, or later a reincarnation of Robin Hood equipped with a bow and a few homemade arrows. People have said that the track was once a section of a Roman road although I never espied a centurion on my way or found an artefact or a Roman coin.

The Romans had been in Wales and certainly in North Breconshire but despite my imaginative searches found no evidence of their presence although Bryn Brynmoelddu found some arrowheads on the farm whilst ploughing. I think they were donated to Cardiff museum.

Above the crossing was a small quarry and above that the perennially beautiful oak woods of the Wennallt so thick with leaves and foliage one could easily get lost in the vicinity unless you knew your way. I exercised my cunning tracking knowledge gleaned from my Buffalo Bill annual so I soon scored a secret path which would lead me over the summit of the hill and down to Penrhiwmoch farm when I would visit Dai and often spend the whole day with him. I even took my father with me one time showing him my secret path and leading him by the hand. A kind of role reversal!

If I turned an immediate left at the crossing the little side road would lead to Danyrallt Villa the home of Mr John Williams and his two spinster sisters Mary Ann and Catherine. They were remarkable, generous to a fault, precise and correct in their manners and old fashioned as well as sweet and kind. They doted on me. I was the preacher's son and I was "rosy cheeks and blue eyes". Mr Williams or Johnny Villa as he was affectionately known by those who knew him in the area, was the grandson of Rev David Williams who had been the minister in the community for over fifty years and is buried at the chapel graveyard. If I continued along this road above the farm of Tanyrallt I would eventually come to a little chapel called Capel Y Rhos which had been built a hundred or so years earlier to serve the thriving farming community. The chapel no longer exists. It was dismantled around ten years ago and there is now no trace of its existence. It is as if it never existed. The whitewashed little wall and the gate all vanished into the past.

Back at the crossing, were I to take the high road so to speak I would pass Tyisaf and then arrive at my father's chapel: Troedrhiwdalar. This building was erected in the eighteenth century and has served the community well. In my childhood days the services were well attended, some people travelling by horseback and stabling the beasts in the adjoining stable which always smelled of horse urine and manure. Above the stable was the school room where the Sunday School took place and later the young people's guild which was led by my father. To enter the school room you had to climb a series of stone steps next to a sloping wall. We naturally as wild boys in the summer of their mischief slid down the stone wall ripping our flannel trousers and bruising our dirty knees. Troedrhiwdalar was a hamlet with only the chapel, a cluster of houses and cottages, no shops, no public house and a blacksmith shop opposite my house where Jim Matthias came twice a week to shoe horses and exchange news and gossip and pass on particular messages.

If I turned right at the crossing, the dirt tracked road would lead along Llanfach to

Cribbarth farm which was a splendid old house erected in the 16th century. On a John Spede map I have of Breconshire, Cribbarth is clearly identified and the map is dated 1603.

So the days passed into weeks and then to months and I was now a fully blown Breconshire boy who not only spoke English, spoke with a rural twang, said "summat" instead of " something "used expressions like "sheep sharin' "boy he's shiftin" and was proudly able to recite the following lines;

"Breconshire born Breconshire bred,
Strong in the arm and weak in the head"

here were other rhymes too that cannot be printed and some that I didn't understand but knew instinctively that I should not dare to repeat them to my parents.

After a few weeks I noticed that Rita was no longer coming to the house to help my mother and I was confused and bewildered at her absence. Had I done something to offend her? Was she not well or had she moved away to get married? The subject was not discussed but slowly it emerged that Rita had contracted an incurable disease and had died. The words appendicitis and tuberculosis were mentioned but the circumstances of her death remain a mystery to me. It was my first realisation that people did not live forever and I coped with it quite well in the way that children do. A child's resilience is extraordinary and fairly soon poor Rita slipped into the past. She is buried in Troedrhiwdalar chapel. I still recall her dark eyes and soft voice and at night as I lay in bed to sleep, the trickling river's tones chanted and gurgled an unfamiliar melody, I remember my father's deep, dark, nicotined voice whispering a goodnight of reassurance telling me to listen to the music of the river as it accompanied me to sleep and that perhaps tomorrow we would go fishing. Rita was nineteen.

****

Chapter Three
Beulah School

As I fan the wood flame of my memory gently breathing on the flickering images that appear, I see the smiling shining faces of childhood phantoms that emerge and then slowly steal away as I gaze into the fires. Memory is hazardous and unreliable, open to misjudgement and dispute, the bread and butter of conjecture and contention. But as I write I see the past only as I recall it and although hazy and wraithlike it is as I choose to remember it.

I cannot pinpoint the exact day of starting at Beulah School but I went willingly with my brother Gareth, escorted by my father pushing his old Hercules "sit up and beg" bicycle. We did not have a family car at that time and so we walked the two and a quarter miles my brother and I taking turns to stand on the pedal of the pushbike. I very quickly familiarised myself with the road and very shortly I knew every nuance of the way: the bends, the dips, the trees, the stones, the trickling brooks, the gorse, the ferns, the daffodils of spring and the hazel nuts of summer. I knew where to find blackberries and secret wild strawberries that grew in abundance in the uncut hedges. There were pheasant, owl, weasel, polecat, and buzzard, flocks of sheep, goat, rabbit, the occasional hare and the curlew. One morning in the holy silence of infancy I witnessed the melancholy cry of the curlew on the moor land area between the Llwyngwrgan turning and Penywaun cottage. All three stopped to listen. I was entranced, my father eyes alerted and smiling but brother Gareth disgruntled and bored stared at the ground. It is the most beautiful bird song I have heard to this day although the curlew seldom returns now to the area, It has, without a doubt, one of the most evocative cries with its gurgled sadness and unending melancholy. My father quietly explained to me the habitat of the bird describing its long beak and the colour of its egg. Later I would discover its nest amongst the rushes and the bracken on the ground. In my father's book of Eggs and Nests of British Birds circa 1951 "A resident species which breeds on moors and heath lands in fairly wild country." I will not dare to argue with that!

Beulah at that time was still a thriving little village with a population of around a hundred, two shops, one of which served as a post office, a visiting butcher, a baker, a cobbler, a carpenter, a wheelwright, a nurse, a tailor, a blacksmith, a pig killer, an undertaker, the chapel the church and the pub called the Carpenters Arms. Llwynmadoc C.P. School to give it its proper title had been built around 1880 by Miss Clara Thomas of Llwynmadoc Estate to benefit the local children and was situated about a quarter of a mile outside the village. It was owned, along with the farms and the village, by the Thomas estate namely Commander Evan Thomas whose family had lived there for several centuries. It was a solidly built stone building with slated roofs, in late Victorian style with two main classrooms on either flank, one for the infants and one for the seniors, and a middle room which served as a dining area, a store room for a meagre collection of books and a place where naughty boys were sent either to cool off or to read quietly. There was also a cloakroom of a kind with pegs on which to hang your coat and a wash basin. There was another room which was, by all accounts, out of bounds where the school cook, Mrs Prosser produced some very healthy and nutritious meals. There was no inside toilet and no electricity. Attached to the school was the school house, a similarly built stone dwelling, very cold and very damp. Each of the three main rooms in the school had an old cast iron piped stove which took an age to warm up, occasionally stifling us with its fumes, but eventually filling the room with warmth. The stoves had to be stoked opening a flap which had the motif of a tortoise and the caption " Slow but sure" As everyone walked to school in those early days there was inevitably an assortment of clothing drying around the stove on a fireguard. We drank cocoa sometimes making it from a large tin that smelled of chocolate. In the middle room was an easel where the attendance number for the day was recorded in white chalk. I seem to recall quite clearly the number 36.

The school was set in an acre of ground untarred and partly comprising a rather boggy outfield with rushes, a stream, a hawthorn hedge and silver birch trees. Many children, particularly the girls would plait the rushes and wear them as decorative pieces of hand made jewellery. There were also two splendid trees at the bottom of the yard: a lime and a beech. There was a hedge and a cast iron kissing gate which improvised an old tune whenever it opened its rusty mouth. At that time educational reform was in its infancy and many children from the farming community stayed in school at Beulah until they were fourteen and did not venture into the secondary school system. As a result, to a five year old infant someone of fourteen was regarded as an adult who not only physically towered over them but lived in a completely alien post pubescent world. There were plenty of teasing and good natured high jinks but seldom any bullying. What you saw is what you got and the older pupils looked after the younger ones with a natural sense of propriety and decency. Besides the more traditional games like football and rounders which were played with gusto and wild determination, there were other activities like "hide and seek", "stuck in the mud" a game where with a pointed stick you tried to collect as many dead leaves as possible, skipping games mostly favoured by the girls and a game called "attention" which involved the throwing of a ball over the roof of the toilet the rules of which are lost in my memory. There was also a game called "I sent a letter to my love" which was open to all ages and both sexes and involved a lot of chasing and was perhaps mildly naughty in its own sweet way. Some of the older boys played with sticks as swords and I was once captured by an older boy "Surrender or die?" he ordered. I didn't know anyone called surrender so I said. "Dai."

I distinctly remember John Claude standing on a "stonk" pretending to read the weather forecast. I can hear him now in his distinctive north Breconshire drawl. "Faeroes.... Fairile... Hebrides.. Malin.." There was also a frenetic game of fox and hounds, all howling, barking and tallyhoing, which inevitably comprised a chase and resulted in bruised bodies, muddy clothes and cut knees. There was another game even more furious and hysterical called "killing the pig" where boys chased and caught another misfortunate and holding him down proceeded to " kill" him whilst the boy himself, usually John Davies from Cilderwen-Jack Cilderry, would scream and howl between gales of laughter and crocodile tears as he quite convincingly portrayed the condemned and pathetic animal. But all the games and entertainment were discharged with good humour and excitement and without the slightest trace of vindictiveness.

Every boy possessed a penknife of some description and not only were they necessities for making swords, daggers and a bow and an arrow, they also prised open locks, carved initials in wood, unearthed buried treasure, cut string for conkers and sometimes if you had the appropriate attachment would bore a hole in the conker in order to put the string through. But John Claude, or to give him his full name: John Raymond Cecil Claude Jones, was the instigator of carving a groove around the circumference of the beech tree at the bottom of the yard. With the assistance of others and taking perhaps a week or two in which to complete the task they eventually succeeded. The indentation was about half an inch wide and a similar size in depth The cutting remained on that tree for many years until nature in its wisdom eventually returned it to its original state.

Beulah school at that time, 1948, had two teachers Miss Blodwen Morgan from Llangammarch who looked after the infants and a young Headmaster, a native of Cefncoed who had been appointed at Llwyn Madoc in 1945 at the end of the war at the ripe old age of twenty one. He was smallish of stature but stern and serious and kept good discipline. He barely taught me as I was too young and I was a little afraid of him then. He would arrive in the morning on a motorbike dressed in a long overcoat and sporting an impressive pair of goggles. We would line up and when the hand bell was rung, usually by an older pupil like Llew Thomas or Olwen Lewis or John Claude's cousin, Margaret, we would dutifully troop in to class. Although I never witnessed it, Mr Bowen would, when necessary, use the cane which would be left hanging at the side of his desk. In general he was well liked by all and sundry but moved on to Penderyn in 1951.

My brother Gareth joined Mr Bowen's class and I was despatched to Miss Morgan's class of infants. She was a kind spectacled lady of indeterminate age, grey haired, sweet, and caring and I fell under her spell immediately making new friends to add to my other pals from Troedrhiwdalar who went to Llanafan School as they lived the other side of the river. Two of my new friends were Derek and Desmond and in a short while, we were known as the three Dees and got up to all manner of mischief. We were all seated in two rows of wooden desks supported by cast iron, the seats being one long bench like apparatus. Miss Morgan sat at her high desk near the stove marking our futile endeavours at writing and arithmetic with a pen and nib which was dipped into an inkwell containing red ink. She made the occasional comment in bold and accurate neat handwriting in our copybooks. I soon learned about the cat who sat on the mat and some odd character called Fluff and that two plus two made four. We also had handcraft where the girls sewed or knitted and the boys drew or created obscure patterns on a piece of paper with the assistance of a potato cut in two. We also learned a few Welsh folk songs which we sang with great enthusiasm and a serious lack of self consciousness which surely intimidated the house martins that resided in the rafters above us .In those very early salad days I can recall two visitors to the school. Nurse Davies who lived in the village and erratically drove a small car was one, She, with a back like a ramrod and her uniform smelling of starch was totally in charge and commandeered us with her inspection which produced a series of giggles, blushes and tears. She would have crossed the steppes of Russia on a camel and put Attila the Hun in his place. The other visitor was Rev Hawkins from Eglwys Oen Duw Church who once tried to entertain us with his conjuring tricks. He made things appear and disappear but brother Gareth was not impressed as he sat on the side and could observe things that others had failed to spot. Gareth was seldom fooled by anything or anybody.

Miss Morgan's role was undoubtedly polymorphous and she had taught at the school for over thirty years. She knew the children very well having taught the parents more than likely and amongst her duties were to administer love and affection, a glass of water now and again and even the extraction of a loose tooth. On the stove she always had a collection of handkerchiefs boiling away as we worked. She also smoked cigarettes. She smoked in the classroom in full view of the children and we regarded this as the

35

norm. I mentioned it to my mother who rather vaguely replied that Miss Morgan smoked because of her health which I found totally baffling but accepted it without a qualm. Occasionally she would send a child out to the middle room in the long afternoon for quiet reading or to complete an unfinished piece of work. I was sent there one day and after a little while I became conscious of another person sitting at my side clutching a book. She had fair hair with an enormous yellow ribbon and a sweet, sad, smiling face. I asked her how old she was and when she replied that she were five I told her that I was five too. I then told her rather shyly that I liked her and she returned the compliment. At that moment I fell in love, a kind of platonic, romantic, idealistic love that has lasted a lifetime and whenever I see her now, a happily married grandmother, she blushes as she smiles.

Perhaps one of the highlights of the school day was dinner time when we all trooped into the dining/middle room and stood in silence at the tables. Grace was said and we all chorused the Amen and sat in hungry anticipation like some street urchins from Oliver Twist. All of a sudden the door would burst open and in would charge Mrs Prosser carrying plates of food and deftly kicking the door closed behind her to retain the heat of the kitchen and to keep out our prying eyes. Back and forth she would step like some minor comic character from a West End farce never failing to provide wonderfully nutritious meals, single handed, and always accurate with her kick of the door. She had an amazing angular style almost like some dance step which totally fascinated me. We had meat and vegetables every day, I don't recall having chips, and the puddings were a gastronomical sensation. We had rolly-polly pudding with custard, prunes, spotted dick, apple tart, rice pudding, sago which was as white as snow and had a dollop of red jam in the middle like a drop of blood on a white sheet. We stirred our spoons in its creating a deep pink mess. We had tapioca pudding which we renamed frogspawn and a chocolate concoction which we very rudely described as black shit.

But undoubtedly for me, the climax of the week was Friday afternoon before Mr Bowen closed the school and set off on his motor cycle to South Wales. This was games time and except for the very young, involved all the children in the school in a very competitive game of rounders and an eighteen a side match of football. This was not a pretty sight with boys of fourteen tackling a five year old girl which at the end of the day resulted in blood, sweat and tears. It was a magic moment when Mr Bowen would lift the latch of the infants room and beckon to the three Dees to step outside to join the bigger children. For me it was as if I was stepping out on to Wembley stadium.

The walk to school was never a chore but more of an exciting adventure and this continued for a few months until the advent of the school car. Gareth and I would begin our trek accompanied by Alwyn next door and amble up the hill stopping for a rest by the towering oak tree. We would continue at our own chosen speed meeting others at the junction to Llwyngwrgan, and run under the skeleton of a tree which we think had been hit by lightning. It was a ghostly sight, a tree of white with no leaves. Then we would proceed past the cottage of Penywaun where we'd be joined perhaps by the children from Cimlelwyd, Penlan, Trefan, Pencrug and Brynmoelddu . Sometimes a little sign would be left to show that the party had already passed and we were not to wait for them. This was in the form of a number of stones placed in a strategic place. Others would join us on the narrow road and we seldom met any strangers, few had a car and even the introduction of the tractor to the hill farmers was in its infancy. We played games as we trundled on our way and I always felt safe and secure with the older children. There was always an abiding sense of solidarity.

After school was over we made the journey back again: Four and a half miles a day for me and more for some of the others. The countryside always had something to show us as we traipsed along. We knew every bird's nest, every wild flower, every secret spring where the water was ice cold and hit the spot between your eyes. As well as games that were played, dares and double dares were thrown at you and I distinctly remember knocking on Miss Edwards's cottage door in response to a challenge from one of the older boys, and asking her if she would care to inspect my most private of parts. The poor lady said nothing and gently closed the door in my face. I am pleased and relieved to say that my fledgling, flashing career came to an abrupt end much to the chagrin of Alwyn and Gareth and one or two others. I also recall falling over on the road and grazing both my knees and cutting the bridge of my nose. I had been trying to follow a certain pattern below me and had stumbled over a stone. I think my mother made me some chips that evening to compensate.

Changes were imminent. Mr Bowen was promoted and was replaced for a short interval by Mr Danny Davies from Llanwrtyd. He was semi retired, genial and slightly deaf, carried a stick which he called Mr Onions and loved music. He once told the three Dees that he could see us behind his back because of our reflections in his glasses. I was naive enough to believe this for many years! Alwyn and his family moved to Llangammarch and the house next door became empty. My sister started school and my brother went to the county. My father, in his long preacher's coat, buckled and belted at the front, brought her in one day to Miss Morgan and I had now moved up to the seniors. She kept looking for him but I was now tacitly given the reins of responsibility which I grasped with both hands. She didn't have to walk to school and never did, even when the snow came and the school car was immobilised. Brother Gareth passed his eleven plus, much to the pleasure and pride of his parents, and started at Builth school with a brand new dark brown leather satchel and the present of a spanking bright new red bicycle: both gifts from his maternal grandfather: Dadcu Alltwen. I was green with envy and forbidden to touch it. I couldn't ride anyway.

The school car was an innovation. David, Tony and Dennis who went to Llanafan school, were taken there by Morwyn Price in his huge old fashioned car which I would see crawling along like some gigantic insect as my sister and I waited for our school car which went in the opposite

39

direction. This was a shooting brake, or certainly an estate car, if my memory serves me correctly of a green colour and was driven very smoothly and not without some style, either by Gerry Jones, Dolaeron or his equally capable wife, Myfanwy. She was cheerful, kindly and humorous and sometimes smoked a cigarette as she drove whilst Gerry was rather serious and sometimes a little grumpy. The car would take the route going from Beulah to Pantycelyn chapel on the Abergwessyn road to collect the children from the uplying smallholdings and then, having delivered them to the school, would come to pick us up after collecting other children from the locality. We loved the experience of being driven and were privileged as others living near the school still had to walk. I remember Ronnie Wilkins starting school. He was a carrot haired little boy of about six whose parents had opened a duck farm adjacent to Penywaun, and lived in nearby Brynoerfel. They had come from East Anglia and Ronnie was a little different to say the least. He sat in the front seat and immediately burst into song, chanting his way to school in a dull monotone repeating some nonsense about "up the leg of a penny". I learned later that somebody had told him that if he stopped singing the car would stop. We, who sat in the back had to suppress our laughter. My sister said. "When I grow up I'm going to drive a car and smoke a cigarette like Myfanwy school car"

The memories of the school are a miscellany and have no chronological order, no real beginning and no real end, and when I remember snippets of incidents they do not necessarily fall in line, such are the distortions of memory. I know that the playground was tarred over at one time and the kissing gate replaced, the toilets renovated and the outside walls of the school clad in thin wood over the grey stone. Thankfully the two tall trees remained as sentinels resplendent in their beauty. But we still had no electricity and only the basic sanitation. Miss Morgan still smoked and we had a new Headmaster: Mr.D.I.Davies. He was young, handsome, smart, bilingual, diligent, chapel minded and a lover of cricket.

The cane was immediately thrown away and the time table rearranged to some degree. For a while I sat at the back of the class with Des behind Pam and Dawn and all kinds of mischief took place. Des would light the fuse and then stand back to watch the fun. It was nothing more serious than pulling Dawn's hair, eating an apple under the desk lid, or undoing Pam's yellow ribbon. I think he brought in a stink bomb at one time...Derek sat at the front a tousled mass of curly brown hair on his broad shoulders, but still managed to compete with me. He was a good footballer, but I was marginally better at cricket, we were equal when it came to throwing a cricket ball, I could sing better than him but when it came to boxing, which we tried only once, I discovered that he produced a very hard left hook. He didn't try boxing with any of the three Dolfan boys! He was elected captain of the Red team and I the Yellow which Mr Davies had astutely introduced. We wore an appropriate band to signify our allegiance and a shield was made from cardboard covered in blue paper. Stars of either yellow or red were then awarded as a member of a house earned them.

Mr Davies encouraged us to read widely, to write creatively and to perform although sadly he could not play the piano which had found its way to the classroom. I read every book that was available to me: Robinson Crusoe, Treasure Island, The Swiss Family Robinson, Westward Ho, Children of the New Forest, Coral Island, Captain Marryat, Lorna Doone which I found very romantic and Gulliver's Travels which I couldn't comprehend and of course Pilgrims Progress which was unexciting and complex but which portrayed another Beulah. I wrote copiously about cowboys and gunslingers, carpetbaggers, pirates and bold buccaneers and was a very sympathetic, misunderstood Herod one Christmas whilst Brian Jones betrayed a very capitalistic streak as a rather belligerent Inn Keeper. I seem to recall Dawn as a rather coy expectant mother awaiting the birth of the saviour. Her portrayal included a very dramatic monologue addressed to the farthest corner of the ceiling rolling her dark eyes when appropriate. Whilst I loved English, I had great difficulty with Maths and found it hard to master the long division. My father showed great patience trying to show me the method whilst brother Gareth snorted with contempt and continued with his Meccano set. Eventually the penny dropped and whilst Gareth could construct wonderful mechanical innovations with pulleys, wheels and string, I could produce only a crucifix, or was it a dagger, by inserting one screw and one nut to two pieces of metal!

We had Geography and History and once a week Hygiene where rather personal questions were asked. Did we bath once a week or was it every fortnight? How often did we brush our teeth? Some children's hands stayed down or they looked absently out of the window. We learned about Africa and the poor pigmy living in mud huts but were happy as they believed in Jesus. We even once, and only once, celebrated Empire Day on May 24th where we stood and stared at the union jack outside in the yard. We were told in some detail about the remarkable journey of Marco Polo and his companions and I won an essay competition organised by Cadbury's about the origins of chocolate, vital information about the cocoa bean, the tse tse fly and The Gold Coast. I have to confess that I was given some assistance by my parents but I proudly still possess a certificate of merit bearing my name although the six bars of assorted chocolate and two tins of cocoa have long since vanished.

On March 1st Welshmen and Welshwomen celebrate St David's day and wear with pride either the daffodil or the leek. When I was a child the day had a greater significance because we were given a half day off from school and the morning was a celebration of Welshness. Mr Davies organised an Eisteddfod in school and we competed in several categories like singing, reciting and creating one's own music. There was also a competition for wearing the longest leek. I'm not certain of our talents but we all joined in with the festivities. Some children created a melody using a comb and paper and I attempted to play the kazoo and made such a mess of it I was asked to go outside to practise. I'd forgotten that one doesn't blow on an "instrument" like that but make a noise through it. I unfortunately managed only to produce a loud farting sound much to the jubilation and merriment of the other children. I won the longest leek competition with the genial help of Mr John Williams the Villa from whose garden it was removed. Other participants in this exercise had failed to control their hunger and their green vegetable had been severely decreased in length and girth by the time the judging took place. There once was a dagger making competition where I had a second prize. The first prize was awarded to Gareth Price although it was not as good as mine. The cold reality was that my father had made mine for me and despite my protestations had continued to carve and polish it until it looked the real thing. I was pleased that Gareth had won. I also recall the determined stubbornness of another boy who flatly refused to compete in any shape or form. He stood in front of the class and shook his head. I don't think he was punished for it.

Treats and outings were very few and far between. Mr Bowen had taken us once on an outing as far as Llanwrtyd to visit the Cambrian Wool factory and for many years I had a piece of cardboard with several pieces of foul smelling bits of wool on it. It was thrown away eventually. We went as a school on a trip to Llangorse Lake and Brecon but it rained all day and the mist was so thick that we failed to see the lake let alone have a boat ride on it. I remember sitting in the back of the bus with Des listening to the rain drumming its hooves on the roof waiting for the weather to improve, which it didn't and passing the time away by thinking of nick names for our school pals. One nickname remains today and I was the instigator. Derek lived in school house at that time and his mother acted as cleaner and caretaker. He became known as "Schooly" and is still known by that name. This was not very original but the others were rechristened but the names didn't stick.

Mr Davies introduced touch rugby on a Friday afternoon and for a while I emulated Bleddyn Williams and Lewis Jones although I knew little of rugby, but my real passion was for cricket. Every year Glamorgan CC would send a team up from Swansea to entertain Builth and I have awe inspiring memories of Wilfred Wooler leading his men as if he were in a test match, barking out instructions and totally in charge. I recall Haydn Davies hooking and pulling shots on to the slates of the houses on the other side of the Garth Road. It was in 1950 that I met Don Shepherd who was at the beginning of his long and illustrious career. He was fielding on the boundary in between overs. He was a delightful man and gave us his time willingly and with modesty. Don Shepherd should have played for England and eventually represented the MCC on an overseas tour. Mr Davies coached us to the best of his ability bringing to the school a bag of cricketing equipment with real stumps and a bat but I'm not certain whether there were pads but it certainly was exciting for the ones who liked cricket. I practised all the strokes that I had read about in the Eagle comic and the Boys Book of Sports and my favourite shots were the backward leg glance and the square cut which I demonstrated time and time again to those most unfortunate to show the slightest interest. Through his coaching and early encouragement I also played a few games for MCC when I was 18 or so. That's Machynlleth Cricket Club by the way.

Mr Davies was opening bat for Builth at that time and usually produced a very good average over the season and I longed to go to see him play and give him my support. One summer I nagged my mother incessantly to go to Builth so that in the end we decided to take the bus one Saturday to see Dai play. She made a pack of black currant jam sandwiches and a flask of tea in a battered old thermos flask, met the bus at the crossing and off we went. I managed to get a seat on the third man boundary despite the capacity crowd of around 45 including the dog! The opposition batted first and although I enjoyed the proceedings and took in as many details as possible explaining to my mother, who knitted fervently throughout, the technicalities of the fielding attack, I eagerly awaited the batting of my hero. Eventually Builth came out to bat. Mr Davies looked particularly dashing in white and a striped cap over his jet black hair. He took guard, a left handed batsman with his bum stuck up in an acute angle and faced the opening bowler. There was a click as the ball tore through his guard and lifted off the bails. D.I. Davies bowled nought. He walked back to the pavilion in utter silence. I bent to tie my shoelaces and discovered I was wearing sandals whilst my mother set her jaw firmly and knitted furiously looking straight ahead. Years later I saw Neil Harvey the great Australian batsman out for a duck at St Helens.

The years slipped by and before I knew it, I was to start at Builth school. I was to leave the security of my primary school with its pictures of the conquest of Everest, a record of Bannister's three minute mile and the print of Napoleon's retreat from Moscow on the classroom walls. When we sang at the end of the day "Now the day is Over" it really was over and a new chapter in my life was about to begin. On that last day, having collected my report in a brown foolscap envelope, I stood by Mr Davies's desk and shook his hand like an old deacon and thanked him sincerely for everything he had done for me. I turned and looked at the old schoolroom for the last time its high ceiling and the old stove, and its wide windows, before turning and walking out the door.

****

Chapter Four
My Father and the Chapel

I never once asked my father why he had entered the ministry and never did I doubt his faith or his unfailing commitment to the word of God. It must have been a difficult decision to make and one which required great sacrifices both financially and socially. I know that he was trained at Brecon Memorial College and that he also spent a year at Swansea University. He very rarely talked of his boyhood days and only the odd occasion would mention some minor incident of his student days. My mother was equally reticent although she remarked on how handsome he had looked when he first preached at her own chapel in Alltwen. I would try to glean some stories or "clecs" from his sisters but there were no skeletons in the cupboard. I ascertained that he had once rooked apples off a tree with another boy called Emlyn Watts, whose son Byron became a childhood pal whenever I stayed at my Grandfather's. My father would also, I'm told, assume the guise of a dog whimpering under the kitchen table so that his younger sisters would feed him with "loshins" and that he once boxed my uncle when their parents were away for the day. My grandfather found out after seeing the scuff marks on the grass and demanded to know what had been going on. He confiscated the boxing gloves and immediately hurled them onto the fire.

When we came to live in Glandulais, father was 38 years old and coming to his prime. He was slightly built, shortish and always immaculately dressed, black haired, parted and cut quite short. Troedrhiwdalar was the main chapel and the focus of his work. Roughly translated, it means the foot of the hill to a headland of a field, although the chapel is about a third of the way up the slope. The chapel was built in the eighteenth century although it is believed that there was a place of worship there in the previous century. There is a large old book of records that was in the possession of the chapel in 1950 and is now in the safe keeping of The National Library of Wales. The records are from 1851 and nothing is recorded before that particular date. At that time the chapel had a total of 248 members and they are all listed in the book. Their professions ranged from farmer, mason, wheelwright, tailor, smith, carpenter, labourer, sawyer, maid servant, miller, shopkeeper, shoemaker, to a fourteen year old mantle maker. There are also records of people from the area who emigrated to America, never to return and I believe there is a Troedrhiwdalar in Delaware county in Ohio. It was in its day a Noncomformist centre of Wales and when Rev David Williams's wife was buried there in 1867 seven hundred people attended the funeral. There was probably an even bigger gathering when the man himself was interred in 1873 at the ripe old age of 95.

My father also served Beulah chapel which had opened in 1822 and Olewydd Chapel in Garth which was erected in 1847. There was also a small chapel in Capel y Rhos where services were held once a month. In my early years there, many old farmers would ride on horseback to attend the services and the stable next to the chapel was well used. Years later when the car took over from the pony the stable still stank of horses and urine. Above the stable was the schoolroom where the Sunday School took place and where later celebrations were held like the entertainment for the Young People's Guild, meeting for The Young Farmers club and the children's Christmas party. It also served as a refreshment area catering for the people who came to the annual eisteddfod in early March.

Chapel was an integral part of the rural way of life then and even in the early nineteen fifties little had changed since Victorian times. Nearly every farm and home was represented in some form or other and some families were very large some amassing a total of over ten siblings. On a Sunday morning the downstairs would be full and only occasionally was the gallery used. There were rows of pews facing the big seat and the pulpit and there were two pews either side of the pulpit, stage right was occupied by my mother and my brother and sister and stage left, so to speak, was reserved for the Protheroe family: Mr John Protheroe, who was the secretary of the chapel and superintendent of the Sunday school, his wife Laura and his brother Rees. The big seat was taken up by the deacons including Mr Protheroe, Mr John Williams The Villa, Mr Davies the precentor and Mr J.J. Jones of Llanafan Farm. There was also another John Williams from Gorse Bank near Llangammarch who rode a white pony to chapel. He was known to us as Williams the white horse.

Because of the proximity of the seating arrangements I had to behave myself as I was in full view of the congregation and I managed to control myself most of the time. It was a double edged sword for I could see the others as well as them seeing me. I remember blushing girls, uncomfortable boys, tall men with tiny wives, tall women with tiny husbands, old men with mouths open as they nodded off, false teeth slipping when singing; Gwyneth Oakfield's piercing soprano and the deep bass voices of Noel Jones, David's father and Vincent Davies Brynieuau. Noel used to wipe his face with the palm of his hand whenever he entered the door of the chapel. I remember the old fashioned clothes worn by the two spinster ladies of the Villa. High Edwardian hats, long coats and fur lined stoles and matching gloves. I remember the oil lamps hanging from the ceiling, watching the lamp turn dark when the wick was too long, the old clock keeping time at the foot of the gallery and the curious concocted odour of polish, hair oil, smoke and moth balls. I remember Bill Jones Oakfield collecting the communion glasses and my helping him. He would secretly slip me a glass of communion wine which was as red as the blood of Christ so I could sample it which I did to my delight. Once an elderly member, having forgotten to adjust his clock when the seasons changed, arrived to the closing hymn, sitting down and taking off his overcoat to receive the benediction! I remember a packet of mint imperials bursting on the wooden floor and rolling like white marbles just as my father was about to begin his sermon. Once my mother in a rush, having busily prepared Sunday dinner before hand, was obliged to keep on her overcoat as she had forgotten to remove her pinafore before leaving the house. She must have been very warm as our seat was very close to the stove. And always, week after week, Ruby Williams accompanied the singing, placidly peddling on the old organ and Mr Davies keeping time.

It was a happy time, a social occasion, an opportunity for some to dress up and Sunday best rang true to its name. Father would preach in both Welsh and English but as the years passed the Welsh became less and less as the younger members did not have a full grasp of the old language.

Then after the service, the chatting outside, or the placing of flowers on a loved one's grave and a smoke outside on the road. Often my father would have a cup of tea with Mrs Price who lived in the tiny cottage close to the chapel called Penrock or Auntie Penrock as she was known. In her small cottage room sometimes there would be more than a dozen people chatting and sipping tea.

There was one time one Sunday morning when I was delegated the tasks of both looking after my sister and to put on the potatoes at around eleven thirty so my mother could have an hour's solace at the service.. I immediately chose to disregard my culinary duty and decided to show my sister my leather holster and "forty five" along with a roll of caps. I deftly demonstrated my quick draw as the caps exploded in a fusillade of fun. We then proceeded to go for a walk up to the chapel to meet my mother. Taking my sister by the hand, I galloped over the bridge on my imaginary palomino with my sister on my back. She was about four at the time and had hardly learned to dress herself. I put my hand on my holster and gun and "rode" to meet my mother coming out of chapel. She was there talking with the ubiquitous Mr John Williams the Villa. "Stick 'em up Johnny" I yelled brandishing my gun grinning from ear to ear. My mother's face was a sunny shade of crimson as she picked up my bedraggled sister who looked as if she'd stepped out of an inner city slum.

In the afternoon we had the Sunday School held in the School room above the stable. This had been a very influential and important asset to the Welsh Victorian way of life. The Sunday school had offered an education to some children, having taught one or two in my time, to learn to read and had helped to preserve the Welsh language over the last century. It was coming to its end when I attended and I have to confess to my shame that I was very naughty in Sunday School! The little children were instructed by young women of the chapel and the older boys and girls were segregated and the boys taught by Mr Jones of Llanafan Farm. He was a fine man, short in stature with neat close cropped grey hair. He was a faithful member of the chapel and was a very serious minded Christian. Sadly, he had little control over us and we all misbehaved. We chatted, swopped stories and exchanged jokes, bantered and wrote secret love letters that were surreptitiously remitted to an unlikely and often unwilling recipient. Generally we paid little attention to our teacher. There was a young girl of about fourteen who played the piano and was very, very pretty. We tried to look up her skirt and at one time we tied her to the chair by her coat tails as she played the piano. For once I was an innocent party but I cannot understand why nobody told my father about this as we caused her deep embarrassment and I think we damaged her coat. We discovered illicit passages in the Bible and read them out aloud whilst Tony, struggling with his reading, confronted the likes of John the Basket and Judas the Chariot. Whilst all this was taking place the deacons sat at a table solemnly discussing the Bible nodding their heads religiously from time to time. Mr J.J. Jones insisted on our learning some of the beautiful psalms and to this day I can recite by heart the 23rd and the 46th at the drop of a hat. There was a time when we boys tried to adorn the breast pocket of our jackets with as many pens as possible. It was at this time when the "biro" first became popular. Later everyone had a pocket watch with which to show off and check the time at regular intervals. I once was reprimanded by Mr Jones as I had smuggled in a rubber dagger which he thought was real. It looked authentic enough and even he was forced to remark. "You should be ashamed of yourself. You the preacher's son." But I wasn't. Ashamed that is, although I was the preacher's son. Then someone in authority had the novel idea of awarding a prize for the best attendance record. I won it one year whilst Dilwyn attained the accolade the following year and after having received his book, never graced the premises again. The books that were awarded as gifts were old fashioned, religious books retelling Bible stories with wonderful illustrations in bold colour. Such titles like Lord of Kings with a most dramatic drawing of Samson in his resplendent glory all bulging muscles and windswept hair but nothing I'm afraid of either Delilah or Jezebel. Not a fleeting glimpse! Then when the last prayer was uttered in unison we would rush through the door and down the steps to play around the graveyard sliding down the wall of the schoolroom and occasionally indulge in a fist fight usually instigated by Glyn Morgan who was an avid admirer of Randolph Turpin. I once reluctantly had to square up to Tony who was half my size and serve me right. He lost his temper and with a face contorted in agony   caught me with a frenzied swing that bloodied my nose and stopped the contest immediately. Then it was tea time.

Often on a Sunday afternoon David or Dennis and sometimes both would come to tea in my house. My brother Gareth would reluctantly condescend to join in with the younger boys but mostly it was Dai and I tucking in to our tinned fruit and thin white bread and butter, sweet tea, Welsh cakes and sponge. After we had scoured my Buffalo Bill annuals, Mother would then play the piano and we would sing under her direction. Dennis hadn't a clue although he tried hard enough. I told mother he would get it eventually if he persisted but mother shook her head. Den was tone deaf. David on the other hand possessed a fine voice and we would rehearse and sing from the Sankey. My mother was a very good sight reader and possessed fathomless patience as she teased a performance from Dai and I. He would get very agitated, shuffle his feet and sniff, get red in the face and often suffer from a bout of hiccoughs but we persisted and eventually some two handed harmony would manifest itself like sunshine bursting through a cloud. My own personal favourites were: What a Friend we have in Jesus, At the Cross, Oh Happy Day and Wonderful Words of Life. Later we would perform in the sacred concert which was held in the chapel in the evening. This was a monthly feature and organised by various young people. I secretly nursed a burning desire to perform and I willingly volunteered to sing A Four Legged Friend with Dai but my request was turned down. I had visions of dressing up as Roy Rogers in full cowboy regalia but I think Dai was a little reluctant to simulate his trusted companion "Trigger."

The sacred concerts were predictable and safe. The same few reliable performers graced the big seat month after month and there were few surprises. There were recitations of a spiritual or moral nature like "Are you Listening in?" and "The Poor Widow" which were performed with great sincerity and to some dramatic effect asking the audience to search his or her own conscience. There were solos and duets mostly from Ira Sankey's collection and sometimes a quartet. Someone always read a portion of scripture followed by a hymn where everyone joined in and the organiser cum compere would always thank everyone at the end and promote the next concert. The pattern of the thank you speech never wavered in its presentation. It was as predictable as night.

"I have come to the end of my programme, and would like to thank all those who have taken part and especially Miss Ruby Williams on the organ. Next month's concert will be organised by..."

My father alternated his services so that sometimes I would go with him to either Beulah or Garth and perhaps hear the same sermon twice. That did not bother me and I recall that my favourite sermon was the Jacob and Esau story. My father called Esau an outlaw and he looked at me from the pulpit when he said this. I was thrilled and embarrassed at the same time although only he and I knew of my admiration for the outcast, the man who lived outside the law. The sad and beautiful hymns that were sung especially at evening when the leaves begin to fall stay within my memory and the haunting refrain of "The Day thou gavest Lord is ended." and the evocative and superlative poetry of Isaac Watts in his "When I survey the wondrous cross" are fine examples. I remember walking with father to Capel Y Rhos chapel hardly bigger than a large lounge set in a wild spot where the dark shadows of trees bent in the wind, a place fit for only ponies and sheep. It was always a special treat for me having him to myself and basking in the glow of his presence and that faint tinge of soap and nicotine. It was always exciting and stimulating to walk in the gathering darkness to this little chapel. It always blew a gale or rained and for some reason to me it was a Golgotha like place having an atmosphere of its own. There was a prayer meeting led by father and in which local deacons were invited to pray. There was a certain theatricality about the process as each man in turn went on his knees and spoke directly to God confessing his sins and asking for forgiveness. They would pray in Welsh which of course I understood and I was always very impressed with Samuel Jones, David's grandfather, who was very powerful on his knees. He would begin in a stage whisper speaking in an almost sotto voice barely audible and very child like, then gradually build up slowly until suddenly he would burst forth like an old evangelist shouting and pleading for mercy to his God and crying real tears. This was not only entertaining to me but also strangely moving and disturbing and almost frighteningly as my senses was assaulted by this tumultuous show of emotion.

In Mid Wales a man is often judged by the size of his funeral and often a little country chapel would be full to overflowing as people displaying their solidarity would come to pay homage to a respected man. In the old days it was said that a farm worker was always allowed time off to attend a funeral and this was an unspoken agreement in his contract so to speak. I have in my possession father's funeral notes dating back to the fifties and one which stands out is that of Daniel Jones of Bwlchciliau. He had been a great man in the area and my father chose as the text on which to deliver his own respect. "There is a prince and great man fallen this day in Israel" Daniel Jones was a charismatic figure and a self taught man skilled in many ways, fond of poetry and able to quote at random the words of many a fine poet. He also had read the Bible from cover to cover having found at first the contents of the Old Testament baffling and intriguing but when he read the New Testament it all made sense to him. In his funeral sermon father compared Daniel Jones to T.Gwyn Jones professor of Welsh literature at Aberystwyth University, observing not only a physical resemblance but having the same intellectual qualities. Daniel Jones had been considered a genius in the district, an avid reader, and a man who had the skills of a veterinary and a man who could be relied upon. I have seen a photograph of him. He had a moustache of two colours, one side white and the other black. He was married to the same woman for fifty years and she bore him seventeen children! In 1952 father buried Mr Evan Jones of Tanyrallt farm, uncle to T Harri Jones the Anglo Welsh poet. Mr Jones was a much respected man in the area. I recall seeing a line of cars parked all the way down from the chapel to our house by the river.

Chapel attendance was a natural phenomenon for me and I never questioned its validity or tried to avoid it. I enjoyed it and loved the idea of belonging to a large greater family where I was loved without concessions and in which everyone was treated equally, with the same respect and the voices of those I loved echo and re-echo in my sub conscious rising and falling like the wayward birds of summer entombed for ever in my memory. Father was always very democratic and very non judgemental to not only us in his immediate family, but also to the people he served so willingly and so respectfully. He was the same to young and old, the intelligent and the slow, in sickness and in health in funeral and in christening. I loved the christening service and here my father really excelled in his cool and steady demeanour. Sometimes the ritual would take place in the chapel after the regular service had concluded. The proud parents would step from their pews to stand proudly but often very self-consciously in the big seat with their infant child clad in white safely held in the mother's arms. Father would say a few words of welcome and offer a short prayer and then take the baby in his own arms, his black hair a contrast to the white of the christening robes, and bless the child whilst the congregation looked on in awe and admiration. He would end the solemnisation by uttering the words of the blessing and kissing the little child on the cheek.

The christening services were sometimes held in private in the comfort of the home and of course we as a family were invited. I enjoyed this because more often than not the baby would have siblings of my age, someone to play with as we darted, dodged and ducked around the farm buildings, scattering the chickens and avoiding the chasing snapping dogs who stared at you insolently with half closed eyes. We were guaranteed a big tea and one of the nicest of invitations I ever heard was "Help yourself Dewi" or "Come on Muster Williams catch holt!" Again being the minister and his family we were often asked out to supper at various farms and one of my earliest memories of this expression of kindness and welcome was on a visit to Mr and Mrs Protheroe at Tyncoed. I must have been about six at the time. At the table I was asked by Laura Protheroe if I possessed a watch. I did not at the time and certainly would not have been able to understand the concept of time but my reply apparently went something along the following lines.
"I have got a watch but I left it at home in case someone stole it."

One of the more pleasant duties that my father had to administer was the marriage service. Often a young couple would come to visit father and he would then spend time alone with them in his study. Over a cup of tea and perhaps a cigarette he would try to advise them of the responsibility that they were taking on and to assist them as much as possible. I was always ushered out of the way when this happened but I had a fair inkling as to what was going on. There was one occasion in early Autumn when a young couple arrived at the house on their bicycles seeking out father. For some reason I was alone in the house awaiting the return of my parents. In my habitual way I invited them in to the kitchen and made them a cup of tea. I decided I would imitate my father but not in his ministerial fashion but in the way he made tea for himself. The kettle was whistling quietly on the fire. I produced two chipped cups and placed some tea leaves into a silver plated strainer that father always used. I reproduced his movements producing a dark liquid as I poured the water over the strainer and squeezing it with a spoon extracted the juice which was drunk with gratitude and an ensuing silence.

Young people got married. Some had to. My mother evaded many an inappropriate question from her inquisitive son who had not yet quite got the grasp of what was going on in the muddled and bewildering field of reproduction at that time. Looking back now from the wisdom of middle age, it was clear that contraception was non existent and not freely available as it is today and when I heard that someone had to get married my first instinct was that her father had ordered her to and that in some most bizarre way she was a reluctant bride. The weddings at the chapel were always a treat. Sometimes if we knew the couple well, we boys would hold a rope across the road and demand pennies from the groom as we "stopped "the car and on one occasion a young man uprooted a five bar gate from the hedge and stood with it in front of the bridal car. The same youth, acting as best man inadvertently dropped the wedding ring which casually rolled under the organ out of sight. My father stood patiently, calm faced as if he were rolling a cigarette or waiting for a bus as the groom and his best pal disappeared on their knees, their suits shining and bulging searching for the elusive band of gold. Another man stood outside the chapel and fired a shotgun into the air frightening the birds and scattering the sheep as he warded off the evil spirits. Sometimes the bride would be late and Ruby would pummel the pedals of the organ repeating the same musical refrain, her face giving nothing away as the congregation glanced over their shoulders in anticipation waiting to hear the scudding of the door and the imminent arrival of the blushing bride who always wore white, never mind the weather and no matter what was the impending situation.

Then in early summer a meeting would be held after Sunday School to decide whether there was going to be a trip to the seaside. Although the outcome was a foregone conclusion, I always hoped we would go to somewhere else but in the end it was nearly always Aberystwyth. Then a date was set and everyone began looking forward to the great day out. I'd start saving any meagre pocket money I could get and be on my best behaviour until eventually the day would arrive and bringing with it hopefully dry and sunny weather. One year we ventured to Barmouth but the journey was so long and so tedious that Aberystwyth became the safe bet and we children didn't mind as there was so much we could do and enjoy.

When the big day dawned, I'd arise with the minimum of fuss and wash at the cold tap in the scullery, splashing water on my curly hair so that I could create a wave to make you sea sick, a quick breakfast and with a packet of home made sandwiches, dressed to kill in short flannel trousers a tank top and sandals I would be ready before anyone else was anywhere near. I'd run to the window to see if any body had already congregated at the crossing to meet the two coaches, courtesy of Sargents Motors Builth Wells. There were always two coaches, forty five seaters, in a dark green colour with upright seats in two rows and a coveted back seat. Who were the drivers? George or Elwyn? When we had decided on the coach we would race for the back seat and there we would sit like young aristocrats on the way to the ball all shining and kitted out for the Sunday School Trip to Aberystwyth.

Eventually after much chatter and the arranging of bags, coats, the occasional bucket and spade and long overcoats and umbrellas, the counting of names and the ticking off on sheets of paper, my father smiling, looking handsome in his suit and clerical collar, we would set off in low gear and start to slowly climb the Dalar pitch past the chapel and the Rhiw down past the neighbouring farms, waving to all and sundry singing as we went, in happy unison, in love with life and all its Sunday school pleasures. And surely as the day is long the sun shone creating pictures on the windows of the coaches with colours of green, turquoise and yellow as we trundled along. Voices, shrill and laced with good humour would ring out above the general hubbub of conversation and the loud roar of the engine.

"Are we nearly there yet?"

"First to see the sea!"

"Give us a wine gum"

"I feel sick"

"Sit down at the back or we will have to stop the bus."

"How much money have you got?" The musical chirping chimes of happy children.

And then Mr Protheroe, in his official capacity as the Chief Superintendant of the Sunday School would make a short speech, his lined face beaming with pleasure and benevolence.

"Dear Christian friends," he'd begin and then at the end of his offering, each child would be given a sixpenny bit to spend. Then the hymn singing would start to help break the journey led again by Mr Protheroe in a rather sedate quaky voice and perhaps John Williams the Villa who loved Aberystwyth and would take a short holiday there every year along with his two spinster sisters. Somewhere over the Plynlimon range and hurtling downwards into Cardiganshire, someone would surely spot the distant sea dancing and shimmering in the morning sun. We'd all rush to the side of the coach to get a glimpse of it and then it would disappear from view hidden by the pine trees of the forestry and the rolling hills. Then slowly but surely like the proverbial tortoise we'd roll and slither, in a gear crashing rhythm into the big car park near the station. Father in his unhurried way would remind everybody when to return to the coach and not to be late and always a gentle reminder to the adult men not to overindulge as far as intoxicating liquor was concerned. And then the day would really begin in earnest.

Firstly we boys, David, Dennis Tony and me would make an early inspection checking to see if the sea was still there. I'd scan the horizons in case there was a pirate ship looming on the Spanish Main just off Aberaeron, slipping into my Gregory Peck as Captain Hornblower guise and then we'd race on to the shingled beach our shoes and sandals disappearing into the soft and sea weed smelling shore. We seldom ventured into the sea as the water was very deep and there is no long stretch of sand at Aberystwyth, For the inexperienced bather one minute you are paddling in six inches of water and then next step and its up to your neck. Terrifying! We were country boys and did all our swimming in the river. Then on to the pier and the amusement arcades spending penny after penny trying our Sunday best to win a cheap prize like a chalky dog or cat and never succeeding to win a packet of cigarettes from a crab like apparatus that dropped your bounty inches from the hole where the prize should have appeared. We would venture to find out just what exactly did the butler see and found to our great indignation a film of crawling ants. Other attractions included a laughing sailor whom I could imitate easily and a haunted house where sinister figures appeared with dripping blood and severed limbs.

Then we'd run to the castle area clutching our candy floss which had a peculiar smell and left a reddish stain on your face and lips, where the view over the sea was quite spectacular. One boy swore he could see Ireland in the distance but that was nudging the economy of truth just a little too far. There was a sculpted figure of a woman looking out to sea waiting for her lost sailor to return. She had long tresses like discarded seaweed which failed to conceal her ample bosom. We scrutinised that piece of sculpture with avid interest and increasing speculation. Then a serious and competitive round of putting on the Castle green brandishing our clubs like spears and striking the ground with sheer frustration when we'd miss a simple putt which resulted in the little white ball rolling out of control down a steep bank. We would then return the implements to the jovial little man who smoked Players Please and appeared to live in the little hut that smelled of wet grass and tobacco. I'd show off and speak Welsh with him much to his twinkling pleasure but none of the boys was impressed. This was followed by a cautious and well balanced walk along the ruined castle walls where now I assumed the role of a Welsh chieftain standing on the ramparts gallantly repelling the foray of the invading English oppressor. This in turn was proceeded by a miscalculated exercise on a machine that printed your name on a piece of cheap metal embossing the letters that you had chosen by turning a heavy metal green painted arrow on a dial of some sort. It was pretty confusing unless you were my brother and the key was not to make a spelling mistake and to leave enough space. But no matter how hard we tried the result was usually a muddled mess and an early example of increasing and infectious dyslexia. We would hoard our pieces of primitive art in our pockets along with the boiled sweets and general rubbish that accumulated therein, later to show our parents or whomsoever was dull enough to show an interest. Later they would be discarded with contempt and disgust.

Then we would proceed to walk the whole length of the promenade avoiding the seagulls who like Battle of Britain pilots would swoop and dive and leave their white stream of excrement on an unlucky visitor.

"Shit for luck" we'd yell, quickly darting a furtive look over our shoulders in case we had been spotted by someone we knew. We'd walk and half run along the wide prom hearing voices with unfamiliar accents, North Walians, South Walians, local Cardies, and sometimes even the nasal vocal inflections of visitors from Wolverhampton and Birmingham. At the end of the promenade where you kicked the iron railings there, a strange and Celtic Aberystwyth custom, we'd pay our sixpence and ride the funicular railway up Constitution Hill once irreverently renamed Constipation Hill. We loved the thrill of stealthily ascending the slope praying that the steel cable would not snap and that we would survive in one piece. Then after reaching the summit finding that the cafe prices were exorbitant we'd wind our way back down dazzled by the sun shimmering on the sea below us and fully aware of the dangers of the cliffs where sea birds chatted and shrieked in the rising wind.

Sometimes we would ride the donkeys on the beach who patiently trudged back and forth all day long on the shingle and stone large ears pricked, docile, half sleeping, gentle and sad creatures. We'd listen to the man, dressed in gumboots and polo necked sweater despite the heat, with a sailors cap who invited you to spend half an hour on the motor boat. He'd stand there bawling out his invitation which I never accepted. And as the sun began to slip along St Georges Channel we would check the time on the King's Hall clock and count our remaining pennies. Then to the high light of our day: Woolworths. In those days you could buy quite a substantial amount of junk for a trivial amount of money. Off we would go circling the various counters where bored and disinterested looking girls stood, inspecting the goods and selecting our little purchases. A pencil with a note book, a box of crayons or a cowboy magazine, a funny hat and a whistle, perhaps a multi coloured windmill and once a cricket game with a dice along with a scorebook where I filled in the names of my imaginary team. Llanafan beat the visiting Aussies that particular year. By an innings and four hundred runs to boot.

Then in the gathering dusk we would trudge and traipse back to the car park, sun burned and dusty, thirsty for pop and smelling of the sea, we would relocate the coaches where the mothers awaited the return of their prodigal with fish and chips that ran with vinegar and left dark print stains on your sweaty fingers. Then slowly on to the coaches now not worrying at all about the back seat which was certainly accommodated by older youths, boys and girls who had paired off with each other. We would grin at this but not knowing for certain the reason why. The long drive back was slow and tiring and we tried not to succumb to sleep telling each other stories of the day and swapping presents and other little jewels of junk that we had acquired like a foul smelling piece of sea weed, or a curiously shaped shell or perhaps a naughty post card portraying a busty blonde woman and a tiny helpless little man. One boy cried wanting to return to the sea as he had never seen it before in all its wonder and slowly and deliberately the lights of Aberystwyth were quietly replaced by the dark blue of the ascending night as we crossed the Cambrian mountain range and headed homeward. Perhaps we'd all start to sing "Black Hills of Dakota" substituting Dakota with Llanafan but the weariness would defeat us and there would remain the numbing silence. There were muted cries of goodnight as each family was safely despatched at various points on the way, and home at last to the privacy of my little room. As I lay in bed that night and the moon rose over the Wennallt I could hear the distant crashing of the waves, the cries of the gulls and I pictured in my mind the hordes of people that thronged to the sea side that day, moving rolling marbles that shone, winked and sparkled until the warm and secure silence of the night engulfed me and I sailed my motor boat to sleep.

So my father became an integral part of the community serving its people in the only way he knew. Sincere and honest, unambitious and minimalist, happy to write poems in private, create wonderful sermons that were produced to order, share with the people their simple joys and tribulations. Once at Pentrebach, father visiting a sick member of the family was interrupted when a cow was about to give birth. All hands to the pump and especially when it was discovered that the cow was about to produce twins. Father immediately took off his coat rolled up his sleeves and joined the others in the pale light of the cowshed.

"Your father..he be one of us...." I was told on more than one occasion. He was their last minister never to be replaced. He was my father too.

****

Chapter Five
The Hidden Canyon

In my halcyon, childhood days we were not privileged with the likes of Television and video recorders. There were no refrigerators, no modern technology and not even electricity in our homes. Most of the farms were almost primitive as far as sanitation was concerned, no modern plumbing and a nearby well was normally the source of fresh water. Only a few owned a car, and then it was usually an old second hand one. Farmers still utilised the horse but slowly but surely the tractor invaded our quiet and serene lives. The Fordson Major and the Ferguson were the two popular makes allocated and I soon became able to differentiate between their engine sounds. Whenever we as children heard the sound of a passing vehicle we would rush to the roadside verges and gape like village idiots at the sight, often open mouthed and waving a tiny hand. Now and again a car would have great difficulty ascending the pitch and I once earned a sixpence through offering roadside assistance to a visiting vicar pushing his car to crawl up the hill. Our entertainment and recreation therefore was minimal and more often than not we relied on our own imagination, took our cues from others around us, snatched and grabbed at any inspiration that we could find and proceeded in earnest.

"The Hidden Canyon" was an original idea of mine but my creative juices had been induced by my love for the Western genre and my avid reading of Buffalo Bill's Wild West Annuals. I have always held a fascination for the old western myths, loved the cowboy stories, the old frontier songs like Streets of Laredo and, with the exception of Myfanwy, the saddest song I have ever heard is Red River Valley. With regard to Hollywood's perpetuation of the old west, I had seen Warpath, The Lawless Breed and a film called Texans Never Cry starring Gene Autry who had a lopsided grin, sang in a light tenor, usually slightly out of tune and appeared more at home in equine company than that of a pretty girl. There was another movie in flickering black and white about a boy, his pony and a new rifle that had been given to him by his dad. It was called Roughshod and provided the usual ingredients of good overcoming evil through a fist fight, a shootout and a predictable happy ending at the final reel. Added to all of this, whenever my father had a preaching assignment that took him away from home he would always bring back little gifts to we three children and mine was invariably a Western comic with the likes of Monte Hale, Buck Jones, Lash Larue or Rocky Lane. Once on a visit to South Wales, one of my Aunts bought me a little leather holster in Swansea market which I adored. It was crudely fashioned but made of real leather which emitted a special aroma when you held it close to your face. In it I nestled my Lone Star colt 44 made of blue metal which I immediately painted black. Real hard men wouldn't wear a gun of blue metal. It still works today although I hung up my gun, so to speak, at the age of eleven or twelve. As I scrutinise it now I see two notches on the handle just below the carving of a piebald head, and my initials and 1952 scratched on its plastic coated surface. I don't recall the two bad men I had outgunned that particular year to attain the said notches, but I'm adamant that they had deserved their fate! The toy pistol looked authentic enough and when it fired the chamber revolved.

My early knowledge of geography was gained from the Buffalo Bill annuals and even today I can identify the Western states as easily as falling off a log. The publications were the work of Arthur Groom and illustrated by Denis McLoughlin. His vivid coloured embellishments were spine tingling and unquestionably ignited my imagination and consciousness. I was gripped by a series of drawings under the title of "Names that made Western History" which depicted scenes that included Pony Express, Stagecoach, Winchester 73, Colt45 and characters from the old West like Geronimo and Bill Hickok. In one book, dated 1950, there is a double page showing a posse of silhouetted riders with the caption "And now they're all...riding to see...." and over the page "Buffalo Bill's Wild West Show" But in my forever, stirring, imagination, the shadowed figures of the riders were all galloping across the sky, carried along by the gusts of the growing wind as the dusk gathered around my bedroom and the hooves of the mustangs kicked up a billow of stardust and streaked above the clouds in the shadow of the moon that was about to rise.

In my waking hours, I would blacken my chin with a cork that had been lit by a match and narrowing my eyes as I placed on my tousled head a discarded hat of my father's, I would gallop across the bridge creating sparks from my boots and head for the Wennallt. The surrounding countryside became my open range. The little river Dulas was in my childish eyes, the Rio Grande, the Powder River or even the mighty Mississippi and the irregular outline of a track at the back of the house that led to Cimlelwyd was the Owlhoot Trail where sometimes a real owl would hoot in the dark fathoms of the long night calling eerily from a gnarled and twisted oak. The grey, purple and yellow gorse filled hills above the Ciliau were the Rocky Mountains or the Sierra Nevada where wild bands of desperadoes roamed and waited in the unholy silence. Often on a Saturday morning I would go to Cimlelwyd to procure a pound of butter from the genial lady Mrs Edwards whose daughter Hazel was at school with me. As I journeyed there and back, I was a rider with the Pony Express fighting off the marauding redskins, ducking under a storm of screaming arrows as I galloped and veered both one way then another firing over my shoulder as my horse, eyes ablaze with fear, mane flashing in the morning sun, galloped relentlessly on. Another character that I created was Captain Jim Burly of the US Cavalry or as Tony would have it, the Calvary. Jim Burley a quiet brooding figure, a kind of Celtic Sterling Hayden ,would be in charge of all things that took place in the field behind the house and was a veteran of many an Indian campaign.

Then to the Hidden Canyon: This was a clutch of rocks on a hill above Tyisaf where there was a picture postcard view of my house and outbuildings and the river shimmering in the eternal sun. Over the rocks hung two small oak trees and here we created a hideout made out of branches, twigs, grass and bracken. To enter the little hideout you had to hang from a branch and ease your way down into the darkness. I named it: The Hidden Canyon. I was the undisputed leader of the gang. We were renegades and showed no mercy. We had robbed banks and trains and now were living outside the law, nursing our wounds, existing on bacon and beans, counting our money and planning our next job which was the bank in Tombstone Llanafan. I was known as Billy the Kid, Dennis was given the handle of Sam, David was Jake and Tony became Hank. He was sometimes laughingly renamed Dopey Hank. Tony and I were the only ones to have a gun and I secretly envied his prized possession of a Winchester 73. It looked just like the real thing. Dennis wasn't really interested, used to the company of his older brothers he much preferred to have a secret smoke whilst David was not always able to leave the farm as there was always an abundance of work to be done and David was an only child. His parents relied on him.

We'd invent and re enact scenarios which resulted in much running around, laughter, shrieks and shooting, hiding, jumping, falling and tying our imaginary steeds near another clump of rocks. We'd climb one particular rock and try to out jump one another. Here we were in more ways than one, on top of the world, a place only fit for the buzzard that circled above us, or was it a vulture that was keeping a wary eye over the drygulched settlers that drove their mule drawn wagons below Tanyrallt. On the rock nobody was recklessly able to jump from the very pinnacle except Tony who succeeded once and once only. Poor Tony who knew no physical fear and nearly always took up a challenge. He may not have been the most intelligent of the gang but he certainly was the bravest. After a sandwich and a drink of pop we'd finish the adventure by having a race from the summit of the hill to the door of Tyisaf about three hundred yards away. What lay between us was a rocky slippery slope of moss and grey sharp stone chippings and a mass of green bracken so thick and green. We always called it fern and I didn't know until years later that it was poisonous. We'd take up our positions and at a given signal off we would race tumbling over in our rush, scratching our bare legs, laughing and shouting, whooping like the renegade Indians we had fought earlier in our captive world. The ferns would firstly embrace us and then suddenly engulf us and we would wonder where each competitor was, hearing the crack of a branch, a curse from Tony who was completely lost in the green undergrowth until at last the final dash to the barbed wire fence outside Dennis's house. Red faced and laughing we'd utter our farewells, shriek a final whoop and troop homewards to tea and a covered wagon bed and to lull away the remainder of the night.

Anyone growing up in the post war years would have come under the spell of the Radio, or what we called the wireless. We had an old model firmly planted on the window sill of the living room with two batteries filled with acid on either side. We had the light programme and the Welsh Home service which my brother had marked in pencil on the semi circular shaped dial on the front of the brown, heavy, immovable object. My mother was an early riser and often I would join her as she went about her business and the radio would be turned on. Oh the sounds and songs of mystery that poured from that contraption that would take the listener on an unforgettable trek into uncharted lands and foreign climes. On a Sunday morning there was a country and western type of show which featured someone singing in the style of the great Hank Williams and included guitars and fiddles. Two songs stay within my memory. "I didn't know the gun was loaded" and "Cigarettes and Whiskey." Anyone unfortunate to have visited the manse at that time would have been intrigued and fascinated to witness the preacher's younger son singing and yodelling "Cigareetes and whiskey and wild wild women...drive you crazy...drive you insane."

Then there was a quiet contrast with "Chapel in the Valley" with Sandy McPherson on the organ playing a slow and peaceful melody and speaking in a sonorous and well modulated voice with the faint trace of as Scottish accent. This was followed by the omnibus edition of The Archers. "Morning all, yes it's me Tom Forrest again..." The programme still continues its soapy marathon today although I doubt it is an every day story of country folk. Whenever I hear the familiar opening bars of its theme music I am transported like Jimmy and his magic patch to the warmth and laughter of the living room, with just my mother and me and the comforting smell of Sunday breakfast.

I only just caught the cliff hanging excitement of Dick Barton shouting breathlessly to his sidekick Snowy and experienced merely a whiff of Dan Dare on the ethereal and evanescent Radio Luxembourg. This was my brother's terrain. I was back in cowboy country as I tuned in to Charles Chilton's "Riders of the Range". I was captivated by the sounds of the creaking saddles, bridles and spurs that clinked and jingled along with the echoing shots and whistling bullets that ripped and ricocheted through the radio along with the staccato drumming of the hooves of the eternal rhythmic riders. I remember the announcer boldly stating. "Riders of the Range...with Paul Carpenter as Jeff Arnold, Charles Irwin as Luke....." and at the closing credits the barking of a dog called rustler which we waited for and amused my wide eyed little sister on my mother's knee. We had our own Welsh speaking detective, a kind of Celtic alternative to Dick Barton. He was Gari Trefan and his faithful "cyfaill" Alec. He bombarded my brother and I on the Children's Hour once a week. To the opening strident chords of Tchaikovsky's fifth symphony the announcer would proclaim "S.O.S. Galw Gari Trefan..." (Calling Gary Trevan) and we would be hooked to it in breathless anticipation and the usual climax at the close. For a while Gareth my brother condescended to play with me re enacting the adventures of the intrepid duo...he played Gari of course but the novelty soon wore off as quickly as the programme itself.

There was a hilarious and fast moving comedy show, probably peculiar to the Welsh airways, called "Welsh Rarebit" which made the whole family laugh and had some male character drooling over a girl called Rosie and the shrieking laughter of the cackling comedienne Gladys Morgan. I believe a young Harry Secombe appeared on this programme before attaining fame with the Goons, but I sadly cannot recall hearing him. It was all simple family fun in the true sense of the word and nobody was nasty to each other, there was no bad language and what took place between a man and a woman was their business and certainly not the listener's. In a similar vein was Wilfred Pickles whose broad Yorkshire accent bewildered me as he ordered his wife to "Give him the money Mabel" His programme "Have a Go" was very popular at the time and Mr Pickles would tour the British Isles recording his broadcasts bringing in the people. There were other programmes like Sunday Half Hour and Palm Court which brought a Sunday evening to a close. There was something for all ages. Mother had "Music while you work" which preceded "Mrs Dale's Diary" which began broadcasting in 1948 and continued without interruption until 1969...."I'm worried about Jim." Mrs Dale would proclaim sharing her anxiety with millions of women across the land. My sister would sit and listen to "Listen with Mother" introduced by a posh woman who would ask rather kindly "Are you sitting comfortably? Then I'll begin." Then after a story, a grown man would sing in a crisp well enunciated voice "Tom, Tom the piper's son." And I would burst into ridiculous laughter which irritated both my mother and little sister.

Every Saturday morning I would be glued to the wireless to listen to "Children's Favourites" and the opening theme music of "Puffing Billy" introduced by the genial and kindly Derek McCulloch, or Uncle Mac as he was affectionately known. This was such a simple pleasure and Uncle Mac appeared to appeal to all children. His music was a miscellany of nursery rhymes, current favourites, hymns, serious music and novelties. It's hard to reconcile the fact that young people in those days would have danced to such numbers as "Doggy in the Window" and "In the middle of the House." He played the same selections over and over so they really did become favourites and I suppose that the ones I enjoyed the most were: "Big Rock Candy Mountain", "Whistle my Love"," The ugly Duckling" and "Home on the Range". But in truth I loved them all. It appears that Uncle Mac had been badly wounded in the great war, was rather difficult to work with but had none the less a real love and understanding of children. His approach to the programme was so well pitched that it was not unusual for him to receive two thousand cards a week asking for a record to be played. Uncle Mac first began introducing the programme in 1954 and it ran until June 1967. When he finished his morning show he would appear to speak to me personally when he signed off with "Goodbye children, everywhere." Thousands of others must have shared that sentiment.

I wasn't often frightened by what I heard on the wireless but once there was a play called "The lodger" which was based on the true story of Jack The Ripper. I recall listening to the sounds of the London streets, the cobbled stones, the cabs led by horses and the echoing footsteps of the man arriving back at his lodgings. I was so engrossed by the drama that I was reluctant to go to bed that night. I climbed the uncarpeted stairs with trepidation and as the shadows played on the bedroom wall I was almost afraid to blow out my candle in case the lodger, hooded and mufflered, covered in blood, was waiting for me. In spite of that, the radio still held a fascination for me and again it was Charles Chilton who played the leading role. He was without doubt the true protagonist and he excelled with his wonderful and thrilling futuristic story of "Journey into Space".

This serial ran for over sixty episodes during the middle fifties and when first broadcast was only intended to be an eight week serial. We as a family would take up our seats near the radio listening to Jet Morgan and his crew as they accomplished their landing on the moon in a story entitled "Operation Luna." Andrew Faulds played Jet Morgan and Guy Kingsley Poynter assumed the role of Doc and the comic but pathetic figure of Lemmy was played by David Kossoff. There was wonderful incidental eerie music, great sound effects and the whole thing moved at a fast and furious pace. The serial was broadcast on a Monday night at seven thirty.

This was followed by a second serial which was slightly longer and was called "The Red Planet" where the intrepid crew travelled on a thirty five million round trip to Mars. This was a much creepier story that scared us to death and would be the topic of conversation the next day on the school bus.

"Air lock open!"

"Orders must be obeyed without question at all times."

"James Edward Whittaker.. born 1886.. died... "

It all seems old hat now and young people are accustomed to special effects and computerised images as the Star Wars stories will exemplify but I am afraid a bit of a dinosaur and can still recall Lemmy's desperate cries for help that reverberated around the living room and even perhaps David Jacobs landing on Mars and stating in his inimitable way

"Hello there!"

Then there was the sport. Alan Clark commentated on the soccer with phrases like "Up go the heads" and "over the bar and into the crowd" and I would hear the turbulence of the crowd and the dull thud as the ball was booted up field. I supported Blackpool and David vied with Spurs although neither of us had any inkling as to the geographical location of these two clubs. Stanley Matthews was a hero and David admired Alf Ramsey. Strange to think that both men were knighted in later years for their contribution to football. Dennis and I kicked a ball back and forth in the field at the back of the house and I provided the commentary. On Saturday afternoon we would listen to Sports Report with the unmistakable Irish brogue of Eamonn Andrews and "Out of the Blue".

Similarly, David and I would play cricket for hours on two of his fields at Penrhiwmoch which we named the Oval and Lord's. Len Hutton and Fred Trueman were my heroes whilst Denis Compton was admired by David and Tony, knowing nothing about cricket said he liked Jenkins whoever that may have been. Again I would try to imitate the lugubrious but poetical voice of the incomparable John Arlott.

"In comes Jones, hair down in his eyes, sliding on the sheep shit, around the wicket and bowls to Williams who leans on it and lets the ball trickle out onto the off side. No run. Williams, a tall handsome young man, not out one hundred and forty four in his first test against Australia..... "

In reality, Arlott was a master of his craft and I recall with pleasure his description of an Australian bowler by the name of Johnson, or it might have been Johnston who had a very unusual bowling action.

"In comes Johnson, bucking and 'eaving and bowls to Hutton....."

We never seemed to tire as we played on Dai's fields and we ran and chased, argued the toss, batting and bowling with the sun high in the sky and the trees radiant in their green glory watching over us.

One of the most perverse things I shared with my dear father was our mutual love of Boxing but purely from a spectator's point of view. Only a mildly demented person would put on a pair of gloves and try to kill another man in a roped square. It wasn't a confidence he wanted proclaimed around North Breconshire. Father, like a million other Welshmen, had got up early in the morning in August 1937 to listen to the wireless to hear Tommy Farr fight Joe Louis for the World Heavyweight Title. Tommy failed gallantly but became a national hero in the process. In my childhood the boxing commentator was usually Raymond Glenndenning with his handlebar moustache and his R.A.F. officer's cut glass accent; with inter round summaries by W. Barrington Dalby a Toff in the first degree. Around the fire on a winter's night these two men would produce between them the recipe for a degree of drama as they brought to life the ferocity of the ring. I had to remain silent throughout any fight as my father pursed his lips in concentration as the bout progressed. Glendenning made a few mistakes; he would in one breath be describing the colour of a boxer's trunks and the next he would exclaim "Oh he's down!" and invariably Dalby would contradict everything that Glendenning had said. They were a double act.

"In comes Turpin left and right to the body as Robinson sways back on to the ropes. Turpin again left and right , left and right as the bell goes. Turpin's round, over to you Barry"

"Robinson's round!"

You could almost hear the clink of the glass and smell the cigar smoke but he was a shrewd observer and was often correct in his predictions. Once more the sounds that emerged from the wireless painted a picture in my mind. The ridiculous fanfare as the gladiators entered the ring. You could feel the punches as the thuds exploded, the sound of the baying crowd, the slipping and sliding of the boots on the canvas, the rubbing and scorching of the ropes and the sound of the bell to end the round. I remember Turpin winning against the seemingly unbeatable Sugar Ray Robinson defying all the odds that long ago night in 1951. David's headmaster had proclaimed to the class that there would only be one winner. He, like many others, was proved wrong. Later it would be great names like Dai Dower and Howard Winstone that would hold my attention and produce a somewhat paradoxical feeling of pride and contempt within my heart and soul.

So the radio played a crucial role in my childhood development. I was keen to learn, to absorb facts, to make new discoveries and any book or comic that came my way was devoured immediately. In my father's study were numerous volumes, books of all shapes and sizes but mostly they were theological works and Welsh poetry which was and still is, over my head. The room always smelled of damp paper and stale cigarette smoke. On his desk were always several scraps of paper, sentences scrawled in his unique handwriting on backs of envelopes and a collection of black covered note books, a newspaper cutting and odd bits of information.

The first comics I remember reading were The Hotspur and The Rover one of which contained a cowboy story about two characters called Wal Loader and J.A.Slade. These were exchanged with Alwyn next door and then as my sister grew older we all had to share Mickey Mouse which was a Walt Disney production and contained the serialisation of the story of Robin Hood which had recently been made into a film starring Richard Todd as the infamous outlaw. I loved this story and collected the pictures week after week. Eventually the film came to the neighbourhood and my father took my brother and I to Llandrindod Wells to see it. I thought it wonderful, totally identified with Richard Todd who became immediately my favourite actor. I fell instantly in love with Joan Rice and for weeks afterwards I played the part of Robin Hood over and over. I never doubted that I looked anything other than very fetching in an old hat of my mother's and a pheasant's feather stuck in its band.

In 1974 I met Richard Todd in London after having seen him in a play in which he was starring. In my memory he had been a dashing, smiling, handsome Robin Hood and now here he stood: a short, unfriendly, rather patronising former Film Star who hardly wanted to give me the time of day.

"What did you think of the play?" he barked not looking at me at all but seemingly observing something more important across the street. I had hated the play, thought he wasn't terribly good in it and was so disappointed by his attitude towards me who had so loved his portrayal of the outlaw.

"I'm afraid; you'll always be Robin Hood to me."

The comic was soon replaced by the Eagle all colour and gloss but full of useful information. My brother loved the middle pages which had a slant towards science and engineering and showed the reader how things worked. I was of course back in Charles Chilton territory with Riders of the Range and a character called the Black Shadow who wore black gloves to match his wardrobe. Soon afterwards my mother's best gloves went missing! Dan Dare, pilot of the future was on the front of the comic along with a weird little creation called the Mekon but I soon got bored with that. Inside was Luck of the Legion who had a French companion who ate too much and spoke with a strong French accent. There was Harris Tweed, extra special agent and very early on. a schoolboy called Billy Brave who played football and was a most likely of lads. On the back cover was always a story about a religious figure like St Francis of Assisi or one of the early Christian martyrs. Somebody attempted to wean me, unsuccessfully, on to the Children's Newspaper which was in one word- boring! Then when my brother began having piano lessons in Llanwrtyd after Builth school, he would bring home The Lion comic which featured Captain Condor on the front and a detective called Monty Carstairs with a monocle to boot. As well as the Western annuals I possessed sport books and a rather humorous book about Twm Sion Catti a kind of Welsh Robin Hood who had, like his English counterpart been mythologised, and which I found very entertaining.

I have vague memories of a series called the six day trials where a number of motorcyclists would appear from the dark hills above Capel Rhos come whining down the valley, screaming like some escaped banshee, all forty miles an hour, turn at the crossing and disappear in smoke and petrol fumes up the Tyrosser pitch and away. We would look out for coloured signs that would suddenly emerge like aliens and be left at crossroads and junctions pinned to trees and fencing posts. Little coloured discs which obviously meant something to the masked riders but left us dumbfounded. We would hear the sound in the distance and eagerly anticipate their arrival. They rode three types of motorcycle: Norton, an A.J.S and a B.S.A. The latter was translated as: bloody slow article. To add flavour to the spectacle there would be some riders with a sidecar and we'd love to see the passenger "bend out" and showing off on the curving corners. It was far noisier than speedier. My sister and I would copy this on the armchair in the sitting room much to the displeasure of my brother busily studying or building some strange montrosity.

A highlight of the local people's self generated entertainment was represented in the Young People's Guild. Because of my position as the son of the manse I was able to join the guilds at Troedrhiwdalar and at Beulah. The guild had been instigated as early as 1919 and father was appointed President on his arrival as the minister for the area. The ethos of the organisation was to promote the intellectual as well as the spiritual development of young people and that the programme for each session was to be organised by the committee. There was only one proviso which had a religious allusion and that was that every meeting would begin with a Hymn and close with the benediction.

I have in my souvenirs the membership card for the session between November 1953 and February 1954, and the entertainment consisted of a social arranged by various members, a lecture given by my father, a visit to Beulah Guild who in turn would reciprocate by visiting us, an evening of papers on Biblical subjects, a miscellaneous concert and a competitive meeting. I guess a similar programme of events was arranged in Beulah. Over the few years of childhood the incidents and memories stay within me. I recall Bill Cobbler winning a love letter competition which made the ladies in the audience shriek with laughter. There were challenges where one had to read on sight, an unpunctuated passage of prose which is not an easy task at the best of time. Another competition demanded that you write a telegram using one letter only and I have two examples that my father had recorded in one of his note books:

"Courageous Christmases challenge corrupt communities."

"One ounce of obedience outweighs oceans of opinions."

Mr Alfred Jones of Wylfa in Beulah gave a lecture on Gerald the Welshman which I seemed to enjoy hearing and my own father gave a very interesting talk about W.H. Davies the tramp poet. I have since read Davies's work and realise that he was indeed a great nature poet. Once there was an entertaining lecture by Mr Afan Griffith about his trip to America on the Queen Mary liner. He was very proficient, a natural communicator and he even gave me a postcard photograph of the great ship. I remember asking him if he had met any cowboys which brought a laugh or two from the audience but I was soon nudged from my western realms of fantasy when I was told the size of Texas. I had a vision of the Lone Star state as being similar in size to Brecon or even Aberystwyth and in my innocence was shocked to hear that it was about four times the size of Wales.

Music was everywhere in those days. One of Dennis's brothers had a 78 of "O Mein Papa" by Eddie Calvert which he played on a small wind up gramophone and the needle had to be changed after each play. The chapel was full of fine singers and the local concerts and eisteddfodau encouraged people of all ages to perform. Many could not read music whilst others had a reasonable command of the Sol fah system. We were entertained by the Owen family who played a number of instruments including a mouth organ and a piano accordion. We all joined in with the choruses and once a man from Builth whom I had never seen before, or since, impressed me by singing a little song accompanying himself on the the banjo. It was in a true Music Hall style reminiscent of George Formby or Lonnie Donegan (neither of whom I had heard then) and was probably a little risqué and suggestive. My mother was not very accommodating about it although as usual Father said very little. For days afterwards I would sidle around the house singing aloud "Come pretty one, come pretty one, come, come, come, come." pretending to play a small frying pan in place of a banjo.

Once, and once only, there was a play performed by local people on a small platform in the school room. My mother had a featured role and so did David's mother Orian Jones. For the occasion Mrs Jones dyed her raven black hair with starch, an early shot at method acting, whilst my mother had her lines taped to the inside of a newspaper. The whole play was hilarious from the word go and Mrs Jones opened the proceedings with a line spoken with no trace of Breconshire.

"Quite finished Prue?" which prompted an elderly lady in the audience to remark in a loud voice. "Haven't Orian gone to look old" There was cold tea instead of sherry, lots of bluster and a few prompts and to top it all Elfet Jones appeared dressed as a young woman. Amongst the gales of laughter that greeted his presence I have visions of him tottering unsteadily around the small stage in his sister's high heels, stockings half down, shouting in a high falsetto trying to be heard above the tumult. It was all so innocent and so full of fun.

As well as the guild and its entertainment there was, every March, Capel Rhos Eisteddfod which later became Troedrhiwdalar Eisteddfod. In the afternoon was the children's competition and I entered when I was allowed. I was prohibited whenever Father was an adjudicator but when he wasn't I won reciting "Miss Nan Knockabout" or "Don't stand in the Way." The prizes were always presented in beautifully designed and embroidered prize bags and after the afternoon session there would be tea and refreshments served by the women in the school room where it grew so hot that condensation poured down the windows like rain and the smell of strong tea filled the room.

Then we would attend the evening session taking it all in, sitting high in the gallery watching with great interest the competitors. I loved the old welsh hymn tune competitions where the local men would have a go. This could be sentimentally performed as one or two of the contestants would have earlier ventured into the Carpenters Arms in Beulah or perhaps the Lion in Llanafan. The tune would rise and so would the emotion and this would necessitate a big hand from the audience. I remember Bill Cobbler attempting "Dwy aden colomen." and because he was rather deaf as well as semi invalided would suddenly go off key in mid stream with a flourish and in total abandonment. There would be serious reciters standing there like old barn stormers and one year there were about fourteen competitors in the ladies solo each one singing The Holy City, one after another "Last night as I lay sleeping." But eventually the Choirs would arrive and in reality this is what people wanted to hear. The very soul of Welsh culture. There would be complete silence as the conductor, perhaps Afan Jones, son of the great Daniel, who took his music very seriously, would lift his baton his face contorted in concentration. A great tidal wave of emotion would fill the whole building and then finally it was all over. It was past the witching hour as we all trooped out into the very cold frost bitten night. Walking home was wonderful. There were a million stars in the sky, the air was fresh and cold, and your breath hung in the growing silence, your ears stung from the sudden change of temperature. I'd walk sliding along the icy sides of the road, my torch playing tricks with the bird less trees. Id look up at the heavens and wonder if I could identify the riders galloping behind the moon or to get a glimpse of Jet Morgan and his crew on their long journey to a distant planet. I'd flash my torch into the silver river and even the trout were asleep. In through the door and the silent cold hallway, up the stairs and into bed, whispering a little prayer to my God thanking him for another day. And within a matter of moments too tired to mumble an Amen I'd be asleep.

****

Chapter Six
Father and his Car

In those long ago days of childhood, where everything seemed a luscious green and the sun permanently high in the sky, life was difficult without private transport and the means of getting from one place to another. Sargents Motors in Builth, or to be more precise, Llanelwedd, served the community well with their bus service. We were well acquainted with the local drivers and more importantly they knew us and administered accordingly to our simple needs. There was a bus service on a Monday to transport people to the market and another on a Saturday when people ventured to the Castle cinema to enjoy whatever was showing. A night at the pictures, an evening at the flicks was an adventure with which to end the week. You had no choice but to accept what was on offer whether it was a British war picture, a Hollywood musical, a western or a dour British black and white detective story where the leading man looked like a pensioner in his overcoat and a pipe gripped firmly between clenched teeth. The film stars of the day were Dirk Bogarde and Jean Simmons representing Britain and James Stewart and Doris Day carrying the flag for Hollywood. I recall seeing Appointment in London and later The Glenn Miller Story both good entertainment, sitting on a wooden bench down the front of the small single storey cinema wreathed in smoke and surrounded by courting couples and excitable wide eyed children.

There was a dependable steam train service to Swansea in the South and Shrewsbury in the

North, where the gigantic engine hissed and puffed like some prehistoric animal and where we placed a halfpenny on the rail and collected it later when it had been flattened to twice its normal size. It was inevitable then that my father had to have a car if he were to carry out his ministerial duties to the best of his ability. The poor old bicycle had long since been discarded after my brother Gareth had a serious crash with John Claude when they played one day outside the house. The bike was a write off with the fork damaged beyond repair and the wheel buckled; it was a true case of Hercules unchained. The chapels were all equidistant but to administer to the sick and to travel to various preaching assignments necessitated a car of his own. Father borrowed the money from my grandfather and paid it back over the years buying the model from my mother's brother, my Uncle Glyn. It was a Morris Ten circa 1936, CLR 259. It had two doors, a sloping body, a spare wheel attached to the outside of the boot, coloured black with a blue leathered upholstery, chrome handles and a running board. On the front bonnet it had the motif of the number ten and a picture of a bull or it may have been a ram. It also possessed an incontinent battery, a starting handle which in wayward hands could cause serious damage, a perpetual cough and splutter and in general a mind of its own. But when my mother cleaned the chrome with brasso and polished the black bodywork it gleamed and glittered and looked as impressive as a Rolls Royce and was my father's pride and joy.

We had an apology of a garage made of old wooden slats with two doors, no lock and a roof made of rusting zinc. The doors rattled when you opened them and I used to spend hours kicking a ball against them diving one way then another to stop the rebound honing my goalkeeping skills in the manner of Bert Williams or was it George Farm? Inside, the walls were covered and tacked with rectangular strips of cardboard that father used for insulation purposes and on which were scrawled in a dark pencil which my father called a blacklead, tyre pressure numbers and dates of when he changed the oil, all utterly irrelevant and useless information to anyone other than he.

My father would spend a great deal of his spare time tinkering with the car, adjusting this and that, soldering, mending, sticking bits together, placing silver paper around the plugs, changing a wheel, mending a puncture, assisted with great relish by my brother who had a fair inkling of what went on under the bonnet and how a car worked. I'm afraid it was all a mystery to me, a foreign land, an alien planet so much so that I could not tell the difference between a spaniel and a spanner, could not discriminate between combustion and congestion and could not identify a foot pump from a pair of hob nailed boots. But I eagerly leaned my weight to the back bumper whenever we had to push the beast to start her up. Then there were oil cans, a jerry can for spare petrol and old tyres, bits of tubing, disused batteries and an assortment of ancient tools scattered around in the near vicinity. Because money was always acutely and inevitably very short, most jobs were attempted by Father himself and on the rare occasion where he was defeated he would seek out the assistance, the wisdom and good nature of either of the two men he knew he could trust: Archie Colcum in Builth and Wally Powell in Llanwrtyd.

"Start her up" they would say and with the bonnet open they would listen impassively. Within seconds, like an old family doctor, a diagnosis was made, and usually they were correct. Mr Colcum had a tiny garage near the Smithfield and no job was too small. In those days these men were skilled mechanics and could usually mend the broken parts instead of merely replacing them as is the expensive custom nowadays. The garages always smelled of oil and had rusting bits of iron around the place, posters on the wall advertising their wares, boxes of old screws, nuts and bolts, old tyres and in Wally's garage two children that scrambled furiously around the area on bikes laughing and showing off. I enjoyed visiting Llanwrtyd as it was a good deal smaller than Builth and was quiet and sleepy. Sometimes Father would collect a canister of Calor Gas from the shop on the square swivelling the heavy container clanking and ringing it on the stone pavement as he nudged and cajoled the heavy contraption into the boot of the car.

A journey in the automobile was exciting even to the extent of travelling to Garth on a Friday to collect the weekly shopping. Gareth would bag the front seat but I would have the privilege on the return journey whilst he read the comic sitting in the back. The driver was forever economical, freewheeling down the hill after Cribarth to save petrol and kick starting the old Morris before climbing the incline past Tycoch and then once more freewheeling down the gradient to Garth like some sinister glider silently landing behind enemy lines. My father was a very careful driver, brows concentrated in heavy furrows, thumb poised over the horn in the centre of the steering wheel like an expectant gun fighter, whistling Sibelius's Finlandia under his breath whenever he was nervous but appearing as cool as a polar bear. My brother would challenge him, testing his tolerance by suggesting he drove faster but thirty to thirty five miles per hour was his maximum speed. He would then patiently explain to Gareth the serious consequences of confronting a speed wobble when all control would be lost. Just as well. The road was narrow and bending with an occasional flock of sheep to confront or a drowsy herd of cattle to dodge at milking time. Because he smoked a lot, usually rolling his own in a dexterous fashion, he suffered from a bad chest and would cough loudly in an exaggerated manner and clear his throat sometimes spitting through the open window. One day, to my horror and surprise, he spat his phlegm at the car window which was unfortunately closed. My brother and I watched with suppressed laughter as the mucus slowly oozed down the pane like something out of a horror film. My father quietly and somewhat sheepishly cleared the mess with a handkerchief as my brother and I pretended we had not noticed anything and tried desperately not to giggle. Father may have been a respected and well liked clergyman, a man of honour and dignity, but he was also human, all too human as well.

Sometimes, during school holidays, we would drive to Builth on a Monday for the market, stopping firstly at Garth to fill the old car with a gallon of petrol from a hand pump at Garth Inn manned by a jovial man with a face the colour of brushed plums. Then onwards meeting several cars and stock lorries on the way, waving fervently at people we knew, past Llewelyn's monument at Cilmeri and very excitedly spotting the milestone which proclaimed "One mile to Builth" opposite the farm. The little town was all a bustle on market days with the familiar shops in the vicinity catering for its customers. We would meet many a neighbour and parishioner, farm boys carrying their coats over their shoulder and their caps at an angle on their smiling faces. There was Bradleys, Eadies, Winston Richards, Watts, Downes, Gerald Morris and a tobacconists called Peckham where a sweating little man thanked you repeatedly for your custom and where it was reputed a hot blooded youth could buy something for the weekend. I had no idea what this meant at the time and was more interested in sampling one of the delicious, home- made ice-creams from Conti's cafe. I remember the colours and the noise, the hullabaloo with all going about their business in raincoats and hats and the multi coloured patchwork type shopping bags carried by the women. Groups of people stopped to chat, old men leaning on their forked sticks, dressed in tweeds or corduroys and wearing leather leggings or gaiters, and children pulling at their mother's coats.

"Oh you must be Dewi, or are you Gareth, and how is Edwina..?"

"Well boy, you ave' grown, almost as big as your father."

"Tell me, are you going to be a preacher when you grow up?"

"No I'm going to be a cowboy!" I would reply causing an explosion of laughter.

I could never understand how anyone could mistake me for my brother and was also faintly irritated by the fact that so often they would get my little sister's name wrong. She would be identified as Elvira, Helena, Ellina and any other permutation except Hefina. Her name is not a common name but one invented by my father. She was born in June and the Welsh word for that month is mehefin. My father took away "me" and added an "a". Then a serious inspection at the Castle cinema to scrutinise the photographs of forthcoming films in glossy black and white inside the swing doors, a view from the bridge on the wye in all its glory along the groe and next to the cinema was an old cobblers shop where an elderly man sold "old Stock" and where we got our shiny black wellington boots that lasted a lifetime.

There were also excursions over the Eppynt to Brecon which I adored. Brecon had its own identity with a cathedral, a ruined castle, two cinemas, many shops including Woolworth, a big square, a museum, a barracks and a farrago of accents. I loved crossing over the Eppynt which in my eyes was as wide as the Alps and my father could just as easily have been Hannibal in my immature eyes. This was soon after the war and the ministry still had access to the land. There were signs everywhere of danger, not to travel off the beaten track and there were glimpses of old tanks and armoured cars that had been used for target practice. All tasty morsels to be fed to the glutinous imagination of a growing boy. We would look out for the red flag to signify that firing was taking place, driving past the ruined Storey Arms where the land was bleak and uncompromising, harsh and unrelenting and only a few bewildered and bedraggled sheep sniffed the air. The view from here was stupendous and we often stopped the car, on a slope, to drink in the air and the spectacle. Then farmhouses were picked out and in the distance you could spot the Llanwrtyd vicinity and to the North the cluster of buildings which was Builth. I remember one time we drove through heavy rain and mist and when we reached the summit of the mountain we were literally above the clouds, appearing to be riding on an ocean of white cumulus which was surrealistic and wonderful. After a few seconds I was a fighter pilot, eyes alert to enemy aircraft or in charge of a bomber on a raid over Germany. In Brecon we could look around the shops amongst the winding and narrow hotch-potch of streets and admire the shining cheap goods of Woolworths or explore the ruins of the castle.

My parents were often invited to tea at various farms and small holdings and this became a family affair. Rarely would my mother go without the children but on this occasion we children must have been in school my mother went with father in the car, to a remote farm high in the hills. On the climb to the farm they had to stop the car to open a wooden five bar gate and as my mother got out to do this, the gate apparently opened on its own accord and closed afterwards when the car had passed through. My mother related this story many times but only years later and I was old enough not to be disturbed by its mystery. She would not say where the farm was and now of course as time moves on the mystery deepens. Some things cannot be explained. There are certain places that I visit that even when the summer is at its height and the temperature above the seasonal average, I experience a chill down by back and I find myself inadvertently looking over my shoulder at some unseen presence. I am led to believe that years ago men were hanged at a crossroads for some hideous crime and the corpse left there to dangle as a reminder to other people and once a skeleton was found near a crossroads when men were erecting a new gate post.

Another story that my mother would relate in later years was the one regarding the stranger that came knocking on her door. This was a time when the cottage next door was empty, we children were at school, and my father, absent, busy with his ministerial duties. She answered the door to confront a bearded man in a long brown raincoat and a hat who enquired of her if she had any oil to spare for his pocket watch that he held in his hand. This struck my mother as a rather peculiar request, said she had no such thing, thanked him politely and gently closed the door. She then immediately went to the window peering through the curtains to watch his departure but to her astonishment there was no trace of the figure. There was only one exit route he could have taken but he appeared to have vanished into thin air. Over the next few days she asked if anyone had seen a stranger in the neighbourhood or an unfamiliar car but drew a blank on both requests. Was this a figment of my mother's imagination or was it a ghost that had visited her that day? She was a rather down to earth person and not prone to tall tales or even a vivid imagination. She left the dreaming to my father and his younger son. Again this story was told to me when I was old enough to draw my own conclusions from it. Some things cannot be explained.

So the old car became a familiar and trusted friend if perhaps a rather eccentric and unreliable one. I recall rising before the dawn to travel as a family to Aberystwyth where my father was to be inducted into the Bardic circle. We obviously could not afford to travel the previous day and stay overnight so we had to make the trek in the early hours of the morning. I remember rubbing the sleep from my aching eyes and sitting in my usual place in the back corner seat of the car observing the ghostly world outside. Nothing stirred in the wonderful silence of the new August morning and then as the grey dawn began to break, rabbits appeared on the road, the hedgerows glistened in the morning dew and if we opened the window to invite in the fresh air, the sound of bird song accompanied our festive celebrations. It was all a wonder ploughing over the Plynlimmon and freewheeling rather precariously downwards hearing the wind whistle, towards the sea, following the frontier trail of the Sunday School outings.

It was a proud and precious moment identifying my father and eagerly pointing him out to my wide eyed sister, in his green bardic robes following along in the procession that proceeded sedately towards the castle and where the pageantry of the eisteddfod took place. I remember very little of the day itself other than to share in my father's moment of glory, thrilling to the trumpeted fanfare and the huge sword held in the hand of the arch druid, and feeling inebriated through a cocktail of lack of sleep, the bracing Cardiganshire sea air and the excitement of the whole journey.

There were other journeys which became a tradition in the family and changed very little in its implementation. These were car journeys to the Swansea valley to visit both sets of grand parents. The distance between Troedrhiwdalar and Alltwen is no more than sixty miles but in the nineteen fifties this was a fair distance to drive especially in a car that was prone to throwing a tantrum now and again and in my mind the journey was endless. But I soon became familiar with the landmarks on the way, the places that seemed all to begin with a double L. There was Llanwrtyd, Llandovery, Llandybie and Llandeilo the bends in the road, the litttle humpbacked bridges that turned your stomach over when we crossed them, the white washed little cottages of the Welsh countryside, the clock at Llandeilo, the coal mines near Ammanford and a glimpse of the mountain where my ancestors are buried. Sometimes we would make a detour and drive over the Black Mountain and enjoy the panoramic view and a sudden glimpse of a castle in the shimmering distance. Father would drive, whistling quietly with my mother in the front with my sister on her lap and my brother and I in the back seat arguing and squabbling. As we got nearer to our destination my mother would get more animated and would begin to point out places where a relative lived. This was where my cousin Megan lived, over there was the house of Uncle Maengwyn and here was where John Aeron's father once lived. Her eyes would shine as she spoke lovingly of her relatives and her home town area.

Our first port of call was my mother's home in Alltwen where we would be greeted by the black Labrador called Togo who recognised the car and barked furiously and licked us with his tongue which to me resembled a long piece of unfried bacon. This was the house ruled by my grandfather Lewis or as we called him Dadcu Alltwen. An ex miner, tough as teak, now kept a shop with the celebrated title of WR Lewis, Draper, Grocer and China Dealer. I understood the grocer bit, acknowledged the fact that Uncle Harry ran the drapery department but I did nor comprehend how Dadcu could travel as far as China to make a living. In those early days the house accommodated my Grandfather, my Grandmother, Auntie Miriam my mother's sister, Uncle Harry her English husband and their only child my cousin David Raymond. Added to this was the dog, and my Uncles Glyn and Richard both lived nearby as well as Aunty Mary and Uncle Phil. I worked out that if each one gave me a coin I would be well off going home that night.

The grocer's shop was the front room of the house and was in everything but the name, a typical corner shop that sold practically everything. It was dark and compelling with a magic of its own, a mysterious mixture of aromas that filled the room. There were potatoes in a sack that smelled of earth, rich cheeses that had their own redolence, fresh green vegetables, packets of tea, jars of multi coloured sweets, bars of chocolate in brightly coloured wrapping, sticks of rock, sherbert, liquorice sticks called Spanish, nougat which we all pronounced as nugget, packets of crisps in a pale blue bag which contained fresh salt tightly wrapped in a vivid blue little twist of paper, wooden crates of corona pop, lemonade, and bottles of Vimto and my favourite: Dandelion and Burdock. I remember Dadcu cutting bacon from a red coloured machine and the jangle of the bell when the door of the shop opened. It was Ali Baba personified.

It was a comfortable, well lived in home and I loved sitting in the so called living room where there was a big table on which the meals were ate, a rocking chair with a cushion under which was a miscellany of newspapers and magazines. The Evening Post newspaper carried a whole page advertising what was on in the pictures and I would avidly search through them hoping something exciting would catch my eye. There were back copies of Picture Post with wonderful photographs of recent major events like a Royal occasion or a cup final. There were Welsh newspapers with a theological slant and in total contrast a magazine called Titbits which I thought rather rude and often contained photographs of scantily clad young women which added fuel to my already dubious and furtive imagination. There was also a lovely old oak Grandfather clock which ticked nonchalantly and another timepiece on the wall where two figures emerged to proclaim the weather when it was simpler just to glance out of the window. I have hazy memories of my Grandmother who was known as Mam. She was arthritic, walked with a stick, had bandaged legs, always wore a pinafore and had white hair which complemented her lovely smile. It was at this house where I discovered the taste of coffee for the very first time. A table spoonful of brown liquid was poured into a cup from a small bottle with the words Camp written across it and a picture of a dark man in a turban. Boiling water was added to this concoction to produce a steaming cup of coffee. The taste was disgusting and I stuck to tea or lemonade.

Gareth and I would wander outside to the main road and sit on the pillars of the green painted iron gate watching the world go by. We sometimes collected numbers from the plates of passing cars and we were both intrigued by the red single-decker bus that stopped almost immediately outside the door. The bus would snort to a stop like a wild bison and after a ting ting of the bell, a wave from the driver resplendent in his peaked cap, would roar away in a cloud of clamour, smoke and diesel fumes. I would observe from my look out tower the colliers trudging homewards covered in coal dust their eyes white like a trapped animal caught in some unseen spotlight, scuffing their heavy boots on the pavement. I would see the turban headed housewives with their babies strapped to their bosoms swaddled in warm blankets.

Then we would visit my Aunty Mary and Uncle Phil who lived within walking distance. My mother always warned me not to touch anything and not to go ferreting around in the drawers and cupboards that I was prone to do. They had a nice house with a long sloping garden with fruit trees and where the lawn was cultivated and preserved by my uncle. In their front yard my voice would echo and I would sometimes practise my yodelling skills much to the acute embarrassment of my brother. In the house everything was immaculate and not a cushion out of place. The front room was like a cathedral, all solemn and shining where there was a musical box on which a beautiful ballerina slowly danced and turned to the tinny tune that emerged from within. But in the cellar, where we explored, with or without permission, we would find a treasure trove of things to read, discarded by my two cousins who were considerably older than my brother and I. There were old copies of the Dandy and the Beano with timeless characters like Desperate Dan, Hungry Horace, Lord Snooty and Korky the cat which both my brother and I devoured instantly. Added to this were hard backed books of Just William stories by Richmal Crompton with plots so comical that I would laugh out loud and rush in to share the moment with my mother who was deep in conversation with my Aunt.

Then there would be a change of plan and my father would go across the valley to visit his family. It was an understood thing that I would go with him and Gareth and Hefina stay at Alltwen. After all I was an Alun and my brother was a Lewis. I didn't mind one bit as I would have the front seat to myself and more importantly the undivided attention of my father. He too would become more animated the nearer he got to his own haunts, winding down the little road from Alltwen, pointing out places where he had cycled as a younger man, past woods and over a little bridge with the smoke belching from the works at Clydach and then upwards where the trees started to reappear avoiding the coal mines and arriving at last at my Grandfather's house at Craigcefnparc. Now it was Dadcu Graig, my other grandfather who was the focus of my childish attention He had a shoemaker's shop which was one of the bigger rooms of the large house he owned. I would always try to sneak past his window without him seeing me but I seldom succeeded. He would look up from his work bench, pretending to be startled, peering over his rimless glasses, mouth full of tacks surrounded by all types of footwear. There were shoes of all shape and size of a varied description ranging from a miner's working boot to a rather refined lady's shoe delicate and neat. He was a craftsman and I see him now bent over his work pummelling the leather, shaping, cutting, honing, tapping fastidiously whenever necessary, confident in his craft and an oasis in a sea of discarded cinderellas. Like my other Grandfather, Dadcu Graig ruled with a rod of iron bullying and snorting, sitting at the table in his own high backed chair, hands filthy from his work, scowling at all and sundry, turning occasionally to spit into the fire. I had a job to keep a straight face and I always felt that he was putting it on to keep everyone in their place. I certainly did not fear him although the rest of the family seemed scared witless of him and kept their distance. I would sit, quietly scanning the local paper whilst my father and his own father sat by the fire smoking and talking earnestly. I recall the hand made walking sticks hanging from the stair treads that lead to the upper floor.

Whilst all this took place my Auntie Enid, sleeves rolled up in her pinafore would work like a galley slave, fussing and rushing around the house washing and cleaning always in a hurry. My Grandmother, a quiet and very dignified lady, would move silently around the place, small and delicate with her white hair in a bun, religious, dressed in black, quietly beautiful and serene.

I would excuse myself and step outside to see the little garden with the privy at the end and then to visit the pig that had his sty about fifty yards away. He always greeted me with a snort and a grumble, a bit like my own Dadcu in a way and would have a go at eating anything he was offered. My Auntie Enid would give me a bucket full of potato peelings, bits of left over food and anything which appeared edible. The stench which greeted me was barely tolerable and the old pig would get very excited at the prospect of food, rolling around in the mess which only he had created in the first place. I felt a little sympathy for him, locked up in his sty and knowing that soon he would be slaughtered and ate. I loved bacon and pork chops and soon put the grisly prospect of imminent death out of my mind. Added to the pig were a French Barn and two cows which provided milk and had names which I sadly cannot recall. I would have a little stroll around the field and try to spot the Skewen Steelworks in the distance. Then I would walk along the wall outside the house and back inside I would try to play the old Harmonium with its squeaking pedals, in the front room with little success. Dadcu would then make a big pantomime of offering me a coin. Once, on a previous visit, he had caught me out and I wasn't going to be fooled again.

"What would you like? Gold or silver?" He had inquired.

Naturally I had said gold and instead of giving me a half crown which I would have had accepted eagerly donated a "gold" threepenny bit to my coffers. Now I would say silver and he would look over his glasses and grin like some benevolent Fagin growling and grumbling at the same time.

Then back into the car and return to Alltwen where my family would be waiting for us and my mother would be anxious to leave knowing the journey that lay ahead but at the same time wanting to enjoy the last precious moments with her own family. Then, the climax of the long and glorious visit: a choice of goodies from the shop: Pick anything you want and Auntie Miriam smiling in her benevolence handing out sweets and chocolate like there was no tomorrow. We would troop to the car laden with crisps, chocolate, sweets and a bottle of pop, a comic and a pocketful of coins. Half a crown from Dadcu Alltwen, a similar amount from Uncle Phil, a bob or two from any visiting Uncle, a two shilling piece from Auntie Miriam, a smile from Uncle Harry and a sixpenny bit from Dadcu Graig. With the dog barking furiously and the car surrounded by well wishers hoping the car would start, off we would go on our long and sometimes painful return journey.

We would proceed Northwards from the Swansea valley and as the excitement dwindled and the chatter got quieter I would watch the lights from the innumerable streets ebb and fall and eventually fade away as the countryside loomed ahead of us. On we would proceed as the night grew darker and the car gallantly trundled homewards, my limbs aching and fighting off sleep I would struggle to stay awake before we crossed the Sugarloaf and entered Breconshire before Llanwrtyd. Now only the moon could guide us through the shadow of the hills and the welcoming trees but the gentle purring of the car would lull me into a false sense of sleep and I'd suddenly be jolted into a chill of waking and recognise the familiar and ever loving shape and outline of my home. Now to stay awake in the gathering silence whilst my father ventured into the house to light the lamp seeing his stooping silhouette filling the frame of the window. Then straight to bed, too tired to undress, bewildered in the ambiguity of slumber and into the security of my own bed.

It was not always as straight forward as that. The journey was sometimes an adventure that lasted the whole of the night and crossing the Colorado in a covered wagon might have been easier. Once, I recall leaving Alltwen at what appeared to be the eleventh hour only to find we had a puncture at Gwaun Cae Gurwen. It was so late by this time that we had to wait for a long time before assistance could be found and then I remember playing marbles with a boy of similar age and speaking Welsh with him. After the wheel was changed we then continued only to find at Llandovery another puncture befell upon us. I remember the strange feeling when the old car began to lurch on to one side and I could hear the dull flapping of the dud tyre. There no other alternative but to sleep overnight in the car which I found cramped, cold and very uncomfortable. To add to my discomfort I inadvertently wetted myself and had to sleep in sodden underpants waiting unhappily, in abject silence for the dawn. When finally the cock crowed to greet the new day we trekked around a soporific small town to find a cafe that was open and where I drank a very milky but hot cup of coffee and my mother could use their toilet. I don't remember the cafe or the proprietors only that the people where generous and welcoming and I, dried and fed, was a happier little boy. It was the same little town where we sometimes had delicious tasting chips from a newspaper and the vinegar trickled out of the side and ran onto your clothes. This only occurred when we were early enough and the old car had behaved herself and the tyres had stayed inflated and intact.

My father loved the old car and accepted the challenge of getting from one place to another, rarely exceeding his own speed limit of thirty five miles per hour and always received a salute from Mr Evans who rode along on his AA yellow motorbike and sidecar attired in his uniform. Once my brother had acute toothache and had to be rushed to Mr Capleton in Llandrindod to have the molar removed. That was the one and only time my father sped, exceeding his own limits and hitting the unheard of speed of sixty miles per hour somewhere between Garth and Cilmeri. Finally the old car was sold and replaced by another Morris, DKF 349.I believe it was auctioned somewhere in Gloucester but father had one or two further adventures before she was let out to grass. Travelling back with my mother once he stopped to observe a flowing stream on a hill top, checking it out for a possible future place to fish. He stooped to look over the bridge when a sudden gust of wind removed his preacher's homburg hat propelling it in one majestic swoop into the stream. It took a long time before the headgear was retrieved, a wet pair of feet and a silent wife waiting in the car. Similarly in the darkness of night in the presence of a moon he stopped the car to experience the silence of nature.

"Let's see what its like with the lights out." He casually told my mother. When he tried to restart the car, the battery was as flat and lifeless as a stone! Oh the silence of the night both inside and outside the car!

Several years later in the bloom of my adolescence whilst cycling between Aberdare and Mountain Ash, I came across an abandoned vehicle parked on the busy road. To my utter amazement it was the old Morris looking a little worse for wear but retaining its identity. I could not believe my eyes and tried the door which opened at my turning. I sat there in the driver's seat and stroked the ancient steering wheel recalling all the happy times we had shared together. I felt as if I had met up with an old friend from way back and realised it wasn't a dream because my brother had also seen it. A couple of days later someone had taken her away and the car was never seen again.

****

Top Left - My brother Gareth and I
Top Right - Dressed for school
Bottom - Three innocents

Top Left - A dip in the Dulais
Top Right - Beulah school aged seven
Bottom - My little sister Hefina and I

"Home on the range"

Troedrahiwdalar Chapel 1953

Rev.A.R.Williams

My favourite view (Taken by Gareth 1954)

Winter 1954

Chapter Seven
Home on the Range

Gene Autry warbled it and Bing Crosby
crooned about it and although there were no
deer, no antelope, the stars came out at night in
all their glory, the moon raced across the dark
prairies of sweet slumber and we had sheep:
thousands of them bleating, crying, grunting,
snorting, always chewing and staring at you as
blank as blotting paper. We had foxes which I
never saw but smelled occasionally and which
remained aloof and elusive. There were cows, not
longhorns but a few Jerseys and black and white
Herefords and a raging bull at Tanyrallt which
once broke loose and ran along the river bank
until rescued by Ivor Jones. That day my brother
and I were on a walk to Cefnbran to play with the
boys and we were terrified at the prospect of
confronting the wild bull. We cowered beneath a
hedge above Tanrallt and watched tentatively as
Ivor administered all his self taught matador
skills and quietened down the ferocious beast.
Ivor looped a rope through the ring through the
bull's nose and gently but firmly led him back to
his shed on the farm. There were carrion crows,
buzzards by the score a rare and only an
occasionally glimpsed Kite the nearest to an eagle
who roamed, so they said, the skies above
Abergwessyn where once the wolf had wandered
and had howled at night to the waning moon.
There were stoats, weasels, the odd polecat and
also the tamed ferret that terrorised the rabbit
and was kept as a pet. This was a revolting little
white eyed animal.

We had no goldfish, although I won a replica of the same at the fair only for it to die within days, no dog as my mother hated them and I was nervous in their company but we had a succession of cats that quickly marked out their territory and lounged around our "ranch" as if they were the owner occupiers half asleep with one eye open or licking their bodies with a purposefulness, black as coal and white as snow. They had their usefulness and kept the mice away though sometimes they brought their trophies to the back door where my mother would scream standing aghast and father had to remove the unwanted corpse as the cats looked on grinning evilly at the commotion.

One night my father came home carrying a large cardboard box wrapped in string and lots of holes in the side. We waited in great anticipation, my sister's eyes like two dark saucers as he slowly removed his overcoat placing the box on the table. We could hear the chirping noises as we gradually began to realise he had brought home some chicks. He opened the box, my sister standing on the chair to get a closer look. Tenderly he removed a little blob of yellow fluff attached to two matches which was placed on the floor. The little chick began scurrying around the kitchen flagstones followed by another eleven. Soon there were a dozen golden chicks darting here and there amongst the chair legs and the assorted shoes and feet, looking for food chirping and chattering competing with my sister's wild cries of delight. We caught them all and returned them to the box as they began a new life with us.

The chicks grew rapidly over the next few weeks and soon developed into beautiful hens that clucked and chucked and strutted around the safe haven of our back patio which in effect was soon devoid of any grass and became a dirt track for the contentment of our hens. Rhode Island reds I think they were providing delicious fresh eggs whose yolks were as yellow as corn and sizzled and spat on the frying pan. They were gentle natured birds but could peck your hand if you weren't too careful but occasionally when scared they would freeze and then my sister and I could stroke their backs which were as smooth as silk and velvet and whose colours dipped and bowed in the noon day sun, a motley collection of deep browns red and rust. There was a cockerel who greeted the morning with his cry and swaggered around his roost in all his princely glory head held high red faced and blustering like some retired colonel threatening anyone who would chance to challenge his position.

The poultry was locked up at night in the hen house whose roof I had climbed on several occasions carving my initials on the soft leaded flashings of the sloped roof. I had carved DW loves PJ in large capitals only for them to be discovered some years later much to my acute embarrassment. The fox stayed away and in all the years that I lived in Troedrhiwdalar never saw this animal of mystery, the master of disguise who always seemed to hoodwink his enemy. Ironically I have seen more foxes in North London than in Mid Wales, around the dark alleys and the overflowing dustbins of the vast metropolis. We would relish the meal of fresh chicken when my father had to wring the poor creature's neck much to my dismay. I would look away in revulsion but later tucked in to the white meat on my plate covered in dark gravy. There was the odd accident when one unfortunate little bantam broke one of its legs. My father performed an operation which required strapping the limb together with fishing twine and string. My sister and I stood in attendance like some scene from a film where a difficult and life saving act of mercy took place. The bird survived for a while and hopped around the area like some demented miniature Richard the third and naturally enough became known as Hopalong Cassidy after the famous cowboy character played by William Boyd. When the bird perished a few weeks later unable perhaps to withstand the pressure of being a star, or incapable of leading a normal chicken's life, my brother told astonished fellow schoolboys that Hopalong Cassidy was dead. Had they all removed their schoolcaps in respect failing of course to acknowledge the fact that the late lamented loved one was a chicken?

And so home on the range continued happily and uneventfully absorbing the now well established routines of country life. Very early on in my childhood some men came one morning with axes and saws, ropes and other tools and cut down the beautiful fir trees behind the house. I recall that morning we were all going to South Wales for the day and I only witnessed the topping of the first tree. I remember seeing its proud outline on a blue canopy of summer sky and my eyes filling with tears seeing the tall tree totter and fall with an almighty crash to the ground. I do not know to this day why the men came, why the trees were felled but the landscape changed dramatically with the absence of my friends. One crooked branch had somehow broken off the main trunk and had lodged itself into the ground. For no known reason it was left as it fell and became the natural area for a swing. A thick rope was erected over the sweet smelling and sap sticky bark and it became a playground for the three children and anyone else who joined in. We swung and climbed that rope acting out fantasies concerning pirates climbing and clinging to the rigging and Captain Hornblower standing square shouldered, looking on in total command. Then again it might have been Robin Hood confronting the dastardly sheriff of Nottingham kicking his assailant in the chest and in one movement leaping astride his waiting steed.

Sometimes over breakfast I would hear the Tyrosser boys herding the sheep and shouting instructions to the sheepdog in their own peculiar way. It was such a privilege to witness the unique relationship between a man and his working dog and the skills used by both man and beast. I can hear the cry now in that staccato rhythm of the shouter. "Here baitch..here baitch..get out get out...get out.. get out. Get back...get back   .lie down..damn you dog...here baitch   good girl..good dog" The voice would echo all around the home and the dog would answer and the sheep would bleat and the birds continued to sing. The sheepdog was an animal I could never trust with its sly eyed and wolf like expression when it bared its teeth. I always kept a respectful distance,

I remember going rabbiting with David, his cousins John and Basil, his father Noel Jones and my brother Gareth. I was very young at the time and the memory is not very clear. We were assembled above Penrhiwmoch and it was a bitterly cold and crisp morning the frost still glistening on the mossy bank my feet numb in my wellingtons and my hands aching from the rawness of the day. The oak trees were bare and their old branches gnarled and twisted as if trying to ward off the cold. There were broken branches on the ground grey and half rotten amongst the stone and red Breconshire earth. I was fascinated with the procedure but I think I got in the way much to the irritation of John who took the ritual very seriously whilst his brother hovered in the background smiling. There was a ferret and a net, a piece of wood to hit on the poor rabbit's neck and matches to sometimes smoke the animal out of its burrow. I looked on with a combination of excitement and also a feeling of sympathy for the rabbit. I doubted very much whether I had the stomach to kill the creature but this was all hypothetical as the chance never occurred. Rabbits were both a source of income as well as food on the table but I am afraid I became a hindrance on that day for some reason or other. I remember David having divided loyalty both to his older cousins and to me his friend. Sometimes snares would be left along the pathways to entrap the animals, hand made from hazel twigs and thin almost invisible wire. Occasionally one would come across a revolting iron trap reminiscent of some medieval torture apparatus. I pitied the poor animal caught in one of those but country life is seldom what it appears to be, or as it is so often depicted in colour magazines and the media. I'd see a collection of dead rabbits hanging on the door of the blacksmith's across the road, their bodies already stiffened, the mouths caked with dried blood, their paws lined with orange tinted soil and their eyes glazed and lifeless like the beads in my sister's teddy bear. The dreaded disease of myxomatosis which swept through the country at a frantic pace in the middle fifties put an end to all of that. It was a pitiful sight to see the animals hunched in agony stumbling blindly on the side of the road waiting to be killed. We were told to put these pathetic creatures out of their misery if we confronted them. There was a field down by the river that had always been full of rabbits and with one clap of hands would send them scurrying in all directions with their white tails bobbing and weaving in the evening's glow. I don't think the farmers shed any tears at the demise of the rabbit but the countryside and its way of life was slowly changing, the wheels of evolution cranking and creaking in the process.

My mother, in her later years, would often remind me that in those days in Mid Wales. Money was scarce but we as a family were seldom short of food. Local people continued to be very generous with farm produce and we were also served by shops from Builth and one from Llanwrtyd. Once a week the van from Downes would call selling fruit and vegetables and other various things. I remember the old fashioned scales with weights on the back of the lorry and crates of produce open to the elements. There was a genial and polite man named Mr Hamer who sold groceries as far as I can remember. There was also Gerald Morris from Builth who came around in his van, talking at the top of his voice filling the room with his personality and wonderful sense of humour.

"I'm much obliged Mrs Williams...thank you so much..much obliged."

He was outrageous and funny making we children laugh with his genial teasing and sometimes if time allowed it, sharing a cup of tea with my mother. Then on a Friday night the butcher from Llanwrtyd would call selling fresh meat from a little van, whistling tunelessly and speaking in Welsh. I especially liked his home made sausages which we had as a treat sometimes if we were very good.

We were good most of the time. My brother and I disagreed over most things but we kept our distance. He always wanted to be the boss, so to speak, never calling me by my first name but using the word "boy" or "wuss" and this caused many a fracas but seldom anything more dangerous than a wild swing with a fist and a running for cover followed by a prolonged and lengthy sulk. My mother decided she would have to use a stick on us as was the pattern in homes in the country. She kept a stick above the mirror in the kitchen but never used it although sometimes she would pose a threat waving it above her head like some extra from a Macbeth production and trying not to laugh at the same time. My brother hatched the idea of cutting notches in the stick and then after having suitably provoked her, lighting the fuse so to speak would eagerly await the outcome.

Friday night became bath night. This was quite a ritual in our family. Mother would firstly light the boiler in order to heat the water which would seem an eternity and the tin bath was dragged out. My little sister would go first and when she emerged from the swirling mists of the scullery swathed in towels my brother and I were commandeered to venture into the steaming abyss to await the dread of bathing. We usually had to sit in the used soapy water vacated by my sister and this was a tight squeeze. Pushing, laughing, blowing bubbles, creating noisy and exaggerated farts and screaming when cold water was sloshed into the quagmire we somehow managed to soap our growing bodies. On this particular evening Gareth began to really irritate my mother who threatened to clout him with the stick if he did not behave himself and I observed it all through a closed mouth suppressing my giggles. Eventually my mother lost her temper and stormed out herding us into the relative warmth of the kitchen. She reached for the stick above the fireplace and with one movement swung it through the air only to see the weapon fold like a conjurer's stick before here very eyes to gales of laughter from both Gareth and I. My mother laughed as well knowing full well all along that this was all a silly and childish game. My father sat in his study writing in his notebook and smoking a cigarette whilst all this commotion and hullabaloo took place, But to this day whenever I have a bath I always seem to enter on my knees out of habit I guess having been conditioned by the old tin bath from years ago.

When looking back over childhood, the memories have no order and no priority. Some are clear, others sketchy some almost forgotten and linger in the sub conscious until something prods it or somebody comes along and pulls it willingly or otherwise into the present day. Life was not all milk and honey but we survived to tell the tale. We probably all had measles and chicken pox and I once had tonsillitis which I remember being very painful and once when very tiny I had something or other which necessitated swallowing a tablet the size of a golf ball or so it seemed. I recall my father crushing the tablet, mixing it with jam and spreading it on a piece of bread for me to take. I did. I got better. I once remember a doctor coming in his car one dark and windy night. It was Doctor Fenn from Llanwrtyd who was gentle, kindly and very reliable. I recall his thick moustache, his unfamiliar English accent and his comforting manner. I must have been ill when the school photograph was taken. Mr Davies and Miss Morgan either side of the frame and I, conspicuous in my absence as if I'd never been a member of the school and a part of its way of life.

I came home happily from school one day to find I could not stop scratching my head and my mother immediately dragged me over to the window and closely scrutinised my scalp. She ordered me to stand where I was, cleared the table and spread last week's Western Mail and Brecon Radnor Express over the oil clothed surface. I stood there as if I was waiting for a bus, whistling casually and furtively continuing to rub my fingers through my hair. My mother produced an enamel bowl with an obnoxious smelling liquid contained therein.

"Bend over the table, no nonsense".

I had nits. Little black ant like creatures which were soon scattered along the newspapers and became as redundant as last week's news dead and crushed. Down they tumbled on to the paper to be killed in an instant. A fine toothed comb was applied with great alacrity by my mother and when she was satisfied that the bombing raid over my head had been successfully despatched she then scrubbed my scalp with the foul smelling concoction until my head felt as if I'd fallen into an ocean of stinging nettles. That night I sat by the fire reading my comic in silence feeling very clean and shining whilst my brother smirked in a strange self satisfied way and my sister gazed in wonder at it all.

I had clean hair, washed often by my mother on bath nights and cut on a fairly regular basis by my father. This was a procedure that I hated. Whenever the word haircut was mentioned I'd submerge into a sulky silence that lasted for the duration of the cutting process and long after. The film stars of the day never possessed the haircuts that we country boys had and I wondered why I couldn't look like Gregory Peck or Robert Mitchum. No sense in arguing but to give in quietly and not look in the mirror afterwards. In the winter the ceremony was indoors and private but when the summer came this was something akin to a public hanging and sometimes witnessed by any one passing by or calling to see my father. A chair, it was the electric chair as far as I was concerned, was placed in the yard and a rough towel or old shirt placed loosely around the shoulders of the condemned man and my father would patiently but determinedly set about his business. There was only one style, short back and sides. He would place his hands on my neck and push the towel down the back of my collar and then I would feel the cold steel of the hand clippers on my neck and hear the hated click - click sound. I would have to sit very still, a difficult exercise at the best of times, and endure the agony of his clipping away. Sometimes he would pinch the skin and I would cry out in pain. But this did not deter my father. Clip clip away, the deadwood stage comes to Glandulais. And then the scissors and comb, hairs down my back, ears hot and glowing, neck smarting with the humiliation until at last I was unfettered and liberated....oh the relief and then the constant itch of the fine hairs that would have found their way to the lower regions of my spine. One look in the mirror was all I could muster and my film star dreams disintegrated before me. Despite all of that there was something personal, precious and wonderful about the gentle hands of my father on my head as if he were blessing me, and the faint aroma of nicotine and soap that emanated from him.

My father got on with his work, preaching regularly, visiting the sick and the lonely, giving time to the young people in the area, offering advice and counselling, playing the odd kick around with me and my ball, trying to assist Gareth with Latin, my father had studied Greek, and my mother was always busy with washing, cooking, ironing, sewing and keeping us all clean. She found time to play the piano and coached my brother and I to sing a few old songs on a Sunday afternoon between Sunday school and tea time. My sister was happy in her little world and smiled regularly walking with me or sitting on my shoulders when we crossed a stream. She was well looked after and I only recall her crying when my father came home one day and she would not go near him. He had been to the dentist and all his teeth had been removed: every single one. He came through the front gate his head hanging down a little and when he smiled he looked like something out of the fairy stories my sister read. She hid behind my mother who made a little joke and tried to persuade Hefina to approach him. Eventually all was forgotten and in a matter of days my father sported a perfect set of teeth which made him look a little older but at least he could stand in the pulpit again with his usual quiet confidence and dignity.

One day I came across a bicycle that had been left in the "tentist" across the road and I decided in a rather guilty way to play on it, pushing it and trying to balance on the step. I think it was the property of a young man from Llanafan who had probably ridden it here to meet somebody at the crossing and he would return later to collect it. It was a chance for me to learn to ride and when nobody was looking, I had a go. It was a full sized machine and I had to sit on the cross bar and freewheel before I had the confidence to pedal and keep my balance. In a matter of minutes I discovered to my delight that I could ride a bike. I recall cycling up to the crossing and coming back down the hill as fast as I could and loving the thrill of it, round the corner into the field at the back of the house so I could see my reflection in the back window and my mother laughing and waving. My confidence grew and soon I ventured as far as Llanfach and managed to prise myself on to the seat but only when I free wheeled as I could not reach the pedals. Then the man came, retrieved his bicycle and I wasn't to own a bike of any shape or description until many years later.

We kept chickens. The grass grew on the field and there was no reason to cut it until my father got an idea. He had been brought up in the countryside and was used to a cow and a pig and knew how to use a scythe, a "picle" and a rake. He decided we needed some additions to the family. Hence the arrival of Nancy and Heather. I don't know where they came from but it was a wonderful surprise to me coming home from school one day to be greeted by these two beautiful, gentle and loving females. Two nanny goats: Nancy was the elder, a black and white creature who possessed the loudest bleat you could ever imagine. Later my father would perform his party piece to entertain my sister by reproducing Nancy's roar rolling his eyes and making a funny face. We would all laugh at this seeing the local minister reduced to an end of the pier performer. Heather was more placid, a white skinned animal with a little white beard reminiscent of the drawing of Buffalo Bill in my annual. Both had spiky horns, dreamy, yellow far away look eyes and both would attempt to eat anything. It was not safe to leave anything precious around as the goats would soon chew the object and often ruin it. They were not fussy, wellingtons, shoes, a scarf, a cap or a woolly jumper received the same treatment as a newspaper or comic or even a twig or two. They were kept in the cowshed at night where it was warm and smelled of hay, sawdust and wood chippings and were tethered to an old crowbar during the day which was spent leisurely in eating the fresh succulent grass. We children would sometimes place a hat on the head of the goat and laugh at the silliness of it all to the extent that they would butt you if you persisted in annoying them. My sister would ride on Heather's back as I sang a verse or two of Billy Goat Gruff until the goat let out a little plaintive cry which was a signal to dismount. But in general they were docile and very much loved. My father soon learned how to milk Nancy and I was given a try. The secret was to aim at the bucket, squeeze firmly and fire. It was all fun and joy and soon we were drinking tea laced with goat's milk and in the course of time my mother was able to produce a white cheese which was delicious. Heather, if I recall, produced nothing but she was looked after just as much as her older sister.

One morning in Spring I was playing with a football when I observed my father removing the back seat of the car and lining the area with cardboard and hay. When I asked him what was going on he told me that he was taking Nancy to see the Billy goat up near Rhayader and would I like to help him. I jumped at the chance. Here I was being useful for once, showing an avid interest in something real, not prone to vivid stirrings of my fertile imagination. It was also an opportunity to spend some time with my father. We nursed Nancy into the back of the car bending and twisting the animal until she half crouched in the unfamiliar surroundings shifting and grunting to herself.

The journey captured my fantasy of course for now I was riding shotgun on my father's stagecoach that would take us out far into badman's territory. I narrowed my eyes keeping a wary scrutiny for a sign of the bandits now and again ensuring that Nancy was safe and reasonably secure behind me. Somewhere near Doldowlod we stopped at a small holding and were approached by two men in shirt sleeves and flat caps. Nancy was ushered into a paddock and waited for her lover to appear. Of course I had no inkling as to what was happening and strangely my father did not explain the procedure that was about to take place. The Billy appeared and in a matter of minutes had his wicked way with Nancy much to my puzzlement. I was reassured that he was not hurting her and the men stood around casually but at the ready in case of emergencies. The process was short and to the point and before long we were back on the road, Nancy quiet again in the back and father driving with his usual frowned concentration and me on the look out for desperadoes above the wooded hills of Brynllwyd.

A few months later Nancy gave birth in our out buildings to a beautiful little kid. It was night time and in the shadows created by the flash light held by my brother, amidst the straw and hay and the creaking rafters above where the stars winked Bonzo was born. In a matter of minutes the little kid was on its spindly feet, being licked clean by its proud mother and in next to no time was sucking away lustily enjoying his first taste of milk. What a commotion, what a circus, what a sense of marvel to witness a birth. Father was in his element, eyes shining behind his horn rimmed glasses, sleeves rolled up his sinewy arms and my brother and I gazing in wonder at the whole scene. It was almost Biblical in its scenario, a magic moment. Father cleaned up the dark blue afterbirth, wiped down Nancy, now exhausted lying down in the corner with her little offspring nestled near her, and gently led us out of the warmth of the outhouse. It seemed to me that all that was missing was the Magi and the shepherds and up in the purple sky I sensed I spotted a new shining star that shone so brightly that night.

Bonzo was nothing but a delight. The little animal filled us with pure joy and happiness. He was a light brown and white skinned goat, had a sharp set of teeth and two bumps which would shortly grow into perfect horns. He would bound around the place, licking and sucking your offered finger, tasting everything in sight and prone to imitating a centre forward suddenly leaping into the air and heading an invisible football towards an equally invisible goal. We inspected him daily and observed how swiftly the bumps on his head grew into little horns and much to our dismay he grew up and one day would not play anymore. He would prefer his own company, tethered like his mother and his Aunt, eating with complete disregard to the probing and prompting of the three children. He became an adult goat in the company of strangers. I came home from school one afternoon to find that Bonzo had gone. Sold!
But the adventure continued as Rev Williams had another brainwave. The question arose. Was it possible to raise a lamb with a goat? A "suki" lamb was found, an orphan of the Breconshire storm and my father's experiment was put to the test. Unbelievably Nancy was instigated as the wet nurse to Bambi, hastily named by Hefina, and was as happy as Larry, if you see what I

mean! The wonder of nature never ceases to amaze. The lamb grew fat from a diet of goat's milk and sweet green grass, supplemented by a load of hay courtesy of Jim the Blacksmith and all lived happily together. I recall Gib Lewis passing by the house one day and seeing the fat little lamb remarked.

"You tell your father that I'll shear that lamb for a small barrel of beer and an ounce of tobacco."

I passed this message on and my father grinned and said nothing. The lamb was sold or given away as the case may be but at least he had proved his point and the experiment had worked.

My father was a complex man but was always the minister, a man of the people, despite turning his hand to gardening, fishing, fixing the car, collecting eggs, tapping shoes, playing the piano very badly and playing at being a small farmer. Tony and I were playing by the bridge one early summer afternoon and my father was trimming the hedge using a pair of shears. We looked up to spot a young man of about twenty, thick curly black hair, walking rather unsteadily towards us. We recognised him as a local boy and it was very apparent that he was the worse for wear, smelling strongly of beer. He tottered up to my father and told him in a loud voice.

"I'm a sinnner mustah Williams, a sinner..please pray for me"

He began to cry, quietly weeping staring at his heavy, mud stained boots. My father gently put down the shears, and placing both his hands on the young man's shoulders began to pray The sun was high, the only sound was my father's rich baritone and the murmuring of the river.

The man thanked him, wiped his eyes with the sleeve of his coat and rolled away over the bridge. Tony looked at me with a curious uncomprehending at my apparent embarrassment. But I wasn't. I was proud. I glanced at my father who now had recommenced his clipping of the hedge.

The silence hung heavy on the wind for an instant or two and then the world continued.

****

Chapter Eight
The Pack of Cards

When I look back over those early years and the past is a place designated for visits and not a place in which to live, the familiar, ever smiling faces appear and reappear, rising and falling in a river of memory and like a pack of playing cards that are continually shuffled, each upturned player is a picture card and a winning trump. Indeed there were certainly knaves and villains, probably nasty men breathing hatred and discontent, but they were kept from my sight and walked in other valleys. Memory is selective and discriminating and the people of my glorious childhood, who lived and breathed, were optimistic and ever cheerful, forever smiling, perhaps with gritted teeth, through their tears.

My mother had warned me many times not to say anything remotely unfavourable about anyone in my neighbourhood as invariably they were all related. She may have spoken in jest but she was not far from the truth. There were certainly very large families in existence then and a cursory glance at the telephone directory of North Breconshire will reveal pages upon pages of Jones, Davies, Price, Lewis and so on. In Wales there is no problem with identification as a man is known by his farm or his occupation, or perhaps by a nick name often witty in its creation. Here are some examples. There was a Bryn Brynmoelddu as opposed to Bryn Blacksmith , Bryn Tyrosser or Bryn the Factory. There was Jones Oakfield as opposed to Jones

Dolaeron and so on. Added to the scene was Doug Postman, Rhys Plasterer, Billy Painter, Bill Cobbler, Mike the Coal, Evans the Milk, Arthur Butcher and James Post Office. Pub proprietors were named after their tavern hence Harold the Bear as opposed to Harold the Lamb and Howell from Llywel whose pub had no bar but an open fire with a constantly boiling kettle, a cellar and a cloud of smoke. A John Price working for an insurance company became simply Price Pearl or conversely Pearl Price. A forestry worker was Tomos Trees or Timber Tom, a geologist was John the Rocks, an amateur ornithologist was Sam Chaffinch and there was a Deaf Price, Dai Shop, Dai Twp, Dai Wood, Dai Wheelwright, Dai Click Click the man with loose false teeth and Dai Ack Ack who suffered from a stammer. There was also a miner called Dai eighteen months as he had lost half an ear in an accident! There was a Mr DD Davies known as Dai Cubed, Dai Small Coal from Treorchy, Dai Fag, Dai Spot who sported a large birth mark on his forehead and a man who refused to reveal his middle name who was immediately christened Dai Confidential. There was a huge man called Dai Goliath who once when fielding in the slips in a village cricket match took a catch with one hand whilst rolling a fag with the other. There was one nicknamed Dai Double Yolk after his wife gave birth to twins and there was, and still is, to my knowledge a certain ageless, ubiquitous, infamous gentleman by the name of Mr P. Evans from Porth. I suppose he is as notorious in Wales as a certain Kilroy is in England!

Clergymen were not excluded from the pack despite the genuine respect they were held by most people. There was a Twm Halleluia, Two Gun Morgan who wore a frock coat like a Mississippi gambler, a Jelly Belly who always visited a family at meal times and of course a Rev Evans who became Evans Above. One had to live amongst the people to understand their ways and to comprehend what was going on. There is another tradition in Wales of calling a man by his father's name which adds further to the confusion. Haydn becomes Dick and Martin becomes Reg, Norman becomes Bill and the sins of the father etc.

I lived in Llanwrtyd in later years and confronted these characters face to face so to speak and even though they did not perhaps play an integral part of my childhood development they are still worth remembering. Ronald Davies was a wit and local rhymester who made his living by delivering coal in the neighbourhood. He sometimes introduced himself to visitors as Ronald Coalman, Mid Wales's answer to the great Hollywood star. It was he who was once approached by a stranger and asked if the local pub served decent food.

"I'm sorry I wouldn't know...I'm the local minister and have never stepped inside the place."

He had served his country during the Second World War and one day told me.

"Old Hitler had hoped to have had a dinner in London boy but we stopped him" and then after having paused for a second or two continued... "but I had a good dinner in Berlin."

Moc Thomas had tried to impress a lady visitor by informing her that he was a representative of Crawford's biscuits. Resplendent in a bowler hat and cane he had boasted of his important post within the company. The next day she confronted the same man who was now sporting overalls a flat cap and pushing a barrow of broken stones over the bridge.

"Nice looking biscuits you have there Mr Thomas." She sniffed as she went along her way.

People created their own entertainment and in the local concerts one would see the same routines, the same party piece and they in turn received the same respectful sense of fair play and applause. There were two men of dubious age who sang a duet together. Their choice was always the old Victorian ballad The Keys of Heaven or Madam will you walk. One man who sang with a lovely tenor voice was very short, rather fat and had a red face. His partner was over six feet tall and would play the female role with gusto and wicked humour singing like a boy soprano. You might have bumped into him in the men's toilet when he was changing and it was an incongruous sight to see the well built man dressed in full make up with a roll up drooping from his smiling mouth adjusting his wig before tottering on to the stage in his high heeled shoes. As soon as they appeared and before the accompanist had struck an opening chord, the audience would be hooting with laughter but were nevertheless captivated when either began to sing.

The countryside was full of eccentrics and some were very comical without trying to be funny. Who was the man from Abergwessin who on a Saturday evening would knock on the local Bank manager's house come in and sit down for half an hour watch television before asking "Can I have five pounds please Mr Rees?" It was the same gentleman who not only unaware of banking hours but also had little sense of direction. He had ridden his motorbike to take his test at Llandrindod. He was doing well until the examiner told him to take a certain turning with the result that the examinee got completely flustered and ended up in Rhayader! Sometimes their sense of comedy was underlined with a very strong degree of pathos All very well to laugh at someone who complained about the war in Utopia and the lady who walked home from Builth in a new pair of wellingtons that were still tied together. The pathos ran deep when a man after having moved to the village after having lived alone for so long in his small holding tried to light a fire on the top of his gas stove and only put on the electric light in order to light the oil lamp.

Much mischief and merriment was fuelled by alcohol and the abundant supply of cheap but very strong beer. The stories connected with excess drinking are many and more often than not the so called licensing hours, first introduced during the First World War were either flagrantly flaunted or more often than not totally ignored. Breconshire was not "dry" on a Sunday whereas Carmarthenshire was. Sometimes on a Sunday evening, visitors from far distant places like Llandovery would ensure that the singing from the New Inn in Llanwrtyd was much better than the reedy endeavours which emanated from the chapel across the road from it. Often a man would be barred from the Carpenters Arms in Beulah from being too noisy or belligerent only to return a few weeks later loaded with fresh vegetables as a peace offering sheepishly asking for forgiveness. Some would come out of the tavern at stop tap, the worse for wear to walk home in the moonlight only to discover they were going in the opposite direction! One other local character, a shepherd from a hill farm was known to sleep rough if he had had too much to drink. Forestry workers reported seeing a strange figure emerging like a phoenix from the ashes of a fire they had made burning old bracken on the previous day. He had stumbled and fallen into the smouldering ferns and snug as a bug in a rug with warm cider splashing inside him, had promptly fallen asleep only to be awoken by the morning chatter of the forestry boys.

These were days long before the breathaliser had become law, days when cars were at a premium and high speeds were a thing of the future. People pranged their cars or slid into ditches and only on rare occasions were there any serious accidents. Sometimes one would wake up to find himself still in his vehicle which was lodged in a cluster of hazel nuts and a tangle of briars. One man had called the police and demanded to know who had stolen his steering wheel not realising that he had got into the wrong side of his car. Another had been stopped by a policeman whilst riding his bike home.

"Did you know you haven't got a back light sir?"

"Yes indeed. It's alright mun I'm only going forwards so I don't need one."

A man from a farm in Llanafan, who was very fond of strong drink and became very contentious and noisy when in his cups. He would be seen walking along the road at any hour of the day talking to himself often the worse for drink. One Saturday night after closing time he wanted a bag of chips and stood at the back of the queue in the fish and chip shop in Builth demanding to be served on the spot despite the fact that there were several people before him. The proprietor, very patient and calm put up with this behaviour for a while until finally exasperated took off his apron and called out.

"Now look here. This is no way to behave. Shouting and swearing in front of these people. Look you come around here and I'll be you and I'll show you how to behave."

He led the man around to behind his counter and then began to act out the customer taking his place in the queue.

"Good evening, I'd like a packet of chips please?"

"Not on your life. Get out of my shop and don't come back until you are sober. Next!"

Billy and Jackie were near neighbours living in the countryside between Beulah and Llanwrtyd. They were popular, kindly, generous and hardworking but both enjoyed a drink now and again. I have heard of a of a time that they both lay stretched out on the back seat of the bus travelling from Builth to Llanwrtyd, hiding from Billy's wife in order that they could get perhaps another drink in the village before trundling homewards. Another tale is told of the time Jackie had purchased a new pair of leather braces in Builth on a Monday market day. He and Billy were coming home walking from the main road

147

in the dark of night the worse for wear when Jackie got caught short. The story goes that Jackie was unable to unbutton his new braces and in a state of panic Billy drew out his knife and cut the offending supports thus releasing Jackie from his bonds and allowing the course of nature to take place. In later years when Jackie was unable to ride his bike to town others would see him safely home to his lonely farm house but he would often sleep in the barn as he invariably had forgotten where he had hidden the key to the house. The person would ensure that his matches were taken from him before they left.

The police would, I suppose, make an occasional raid to licensed premises to ensure that after time drinking was not taking place and that the ladder of law had no top or no bottom. On the rare occasion some were held over for the night locked up in a cell to sleep it off. The well worn yarn is told of two men from the locality having been locked up for the night started to shout until one told the other.

"You'd better be quiet boy or they'll send for the police and they will lock us up."

The constabulary did invade the solemn sanctuary a country pub one winter's night in a remote part of the countryside. One after hour's drinking fugitive scampered upstairs to avoid prosecution and in desperation to avoid the clutches of the law dived into a bed fully clothed. The investigating officer noticing a pair of brown boots protruding from beneath the blanket accosted the man and after cautioning him asked him if he had anything to say. The man sat up in his bed in his dark suit and tie and muttered simply.

"Guilty...but insane"

The faces of the characters appear and reappear in the tangle of memory always smiling and laughing with a good natured approach to their lives within the confines of their neighbourhood. David's grandfather was a classic example. In my childhood days Sam Jones was a retired farmer, a widower, who lodged in a house in Beulah. He was a tall very heavily built man, strong as an ox, one of twelve children, close cropped white hair and had been, according to David, a bit of a fighter in his youth. Sam Jones Cefnbran. Despite his outwardly physical and tough image Sam was a very sentimental man, highly religous and a lover of the old Welsh Hymns. He had, I'm told, knocked Peter Price off his bike because he hadn't been to chapel such was his determination to save the young man's soul. Often he would be seen in a local eisteddfod with tears streaming down his face as he listened with unmasked joy to an old tune. He loved funerals, giving my father strict instructions that he was to be buried in Welsh and had told David that he would not die and that his body would rise from the grave after his burial which was a little disconcerting for a ten year old child. Wynne Price the son of Cyril Price the local undertaker had been sent to Korea to fight for democracy but before he went Sam had issued him with the following order.

"You come home safe boy.I will need you to bury me."

There is more to this statement than meets the eye. Cyril Price was a bit of a wag and had been to visit Sam when the old man was laid up with the flu. On the way out from the bedroom Cyril had brought out his measuring tape and had pretended to make a note of Sam's measurements...much to the disapproval of the invalid. He would take offence very easily. He became more eccentric with age, set fire to the ferns above the Rhiw almost causing the fire brigade to be called, fell over breaking Mrs Jones's lamp and driving the newly bought tractor into a fence post which delighted David and made me laugh.

Going through my father's papers recently I came across an account of Mr Sam Jones's funeral at which my father officiated. In it my father had said that the funeral was to take place in Welsh in accordance with Sam's wishes. He is buried in Troedrhiwdalar chapel, Wynne did return safely from Korea, did the business, and as far as I know Sam is still there, six foot under!

We would see him coming from a distance wheeling his old black sit up and beg bicycle with the tools of his trade tied loosely with string around a piece of brown sacking, across the handlebars. He seldom rode the bicycle my father insisting that it was his friend and that he leaned on it now and again for comfort. Enter the character known quite simply as Dafi Bwtchwr, Davey Lewis the pig killer. Some of the children in Beulah were afraid of him and this is quite understandable as he looked quite sinister in his old fashioned clothes, always in black with leather leggings and boots. He had a peculiar manner of speaking, a kind of broken English and a pure beautiful welsh. The handles of his sharp knives protruded from the sacking and his crooked nose and small eyes of his peasant face suggested some indestructible Dickensian character from a previous century. He was unmarried and lived with his sister. Old people would say that he could cross a mountain in the dark of night. He was harmless and illiterate. I was never nervous in his company as I always carried my trump cards up my sleeve. I was Welsh speaking and I was the son of the manse. Although he resided in Beulah, once a month he would visit Capel Rhos chapel for the evening service and he always walked past our house at the bottom of the hill parading his bike and enjoying his walk at about half past four in the afternoon. Had he no concept of time. Could he not ride his bike were questions I asked myself. One day I asked my mother why was Dafi always wheeling his bike and my sister who was about five at the time called out,

"Because it's a push bike of course!"

He came to school once but not to address the class but to kill Idwal's pig. This was the one and only time I witnessed such a barbaric exhibition of cruelty. The pig, sensing his time was up began to cry out in a mournful wailing banshee like call not unlike the dreaded cry of a warning siren. The pig was hauled out from the shadows of his condemned cell struggling, snorting and wailing until tied to the long narrow killing table where he awaited a long and suffering end. A knife would flash in the sunlight immersed into the underbelly and a jet of crimson would flow into the waiting bucket. Gradually the pig's dying call would slowly abate and eventually his eyes would change colour and his mouth lie open and silent. We children watched in awe, some of the farm boys would not bat an eyelid, some of the girls would look away but I was held by the horror in front of me. This was Mr Lewis's trade.

A car passing by met Dafi on the road one day and asked him the way.

"Good day to you. Tell me am I on the right road to Builth?"

"Yes indeed, you are indeed on the right road. But you are pointing the wrong way."

I do not know how true some of these stories are but I heard that someone passing through Beulah in a car had to stop as a funeral was taking place and the road blocked for a few minutes. The driver is supposed to have spoken to Dafi, but it could so easily have been a dozen or so others.

"I was driving through here last week and was stopped because of a funeral. Tell me do they die often here?"

"No. Only once." Was the reply.

In his old age and in the solitary privacy of his own mind he was taught to write his name by the local Headmaster. Wil Rees. Mr Rees had been asked to show him to write his name so that he would be able to sign his will. He did.

Today passing cars and noisy lorries do not stop at the bottom of the hill by the old house. Rarely do the drivers pass a glance at the remains of the old blacksmith shop that stands across the road from my home. It is still there but now merely as a remnant of the old days. I was the fortunate one as I caught the last few traces of a

Victorian way of country life which has now totally vanished. Mr J.O. Mathias was the local blacksmith. Jim Blacksmith or Jim y Gof. He was originally from Pembrokeshire but lived in Beulah where he had a forge and travelled twice a week to his shop here at Glandulais. He came by bicycle at first and I can picture him now free wheeling down the hill with his legs in the air and a wide smile covering his face. Later he was to drive a tiny little car, possibly an Austin7. Despite his trade, he was not a big man. He was short and wiry lean and hard like a light weight boxer and had the broadest of smiles, a waggish sense of humour and a teller of tall tales.

The shop was also small and stood a few yards off the road. It had an outer yard like a French barn where the horses were tethered and where the actual shoeing took place and was known as the "tentis" or perhaps " tentist". I have been unable to trace the origins of such a word. It may have been the place where the apprentices learned their work and hence " tentist" grew from that. This area opened out on to the road and was used often as a pick up point for the delivery of certain goods like barrels of cider or beer. Often on one wall where the wood was old smooth as silk but hard and yellow like new made butter, hung dead rabbits ready for market their bodies cold and stiff. There were initials of long forgotten people carved roughly into the wood and the occasional burn marks from a branding iron that Jim had constructed for a local farmer. This outer area was never locked and was a great place to play football when it rained, to pretend to box on the cobbled floor and in summer to watch the swallows fly in from the outside world swooping and diving in a splash of black and white.

Adjacent to the tentist was the actual forge which was permanently in semi darkness, a faint glimmer of light from the small window where the panes were as dirty as slate, gave the token gesture of light. In one corner stood the bellows and the glowing coals of his small furnace. Nearby was the anvil on which Jim played many a tune ringing out the bells of a new horseshoe, sparks flying everywhere and where his smile gleamed in the brooding darkness. The place was filthy with dust and ash, the taste was acrid, the smell sulphurous and amongst the assortment of tools of his trade, the tongs, pincers, hammers and files; mishaped nails and bits of discarded iron was a trough of grey oily water used too cool the newly made shoe. One had to be careful if he asked you to pass him a tool because often the implement was hot and you burned your hand in an instant. Many young onlookers suffered from Jim's wicked sense of humour except for me who carried his cards in his pocket and whose mother often invited the blacksmith to share our food.

It was an education to see him work. He would trim and cut the hoof of an old shire horse who stood patiently in the open towering over the blacksmith. He would measure and gauge using a specimen shoe and then constructed a shoe hammering it out into a red glowing shape before cooling it abruptly and then nailing it onto the horse's hoof. The smell of burning hoof, the smoke, the sweat of the horse and any other concoction filled the area. Sometimes the horse would urinate and one had to stand well back or else be caught in the torrent of steaming tea coloured piss. Then when the shoe was securely nailed he would polish and smooth the hoof with such delicate precision finishing the job with a flourish wiping his hands on his leather apron.

He was a practical joker, a wag and his own man. One day someone called at his home demanding to see the blacksmith. Jim answered the door lathered in shaving cream and told the man that the blacksmith was not at home that day. He told two boys that there was a circus in Newbridge and how disappointed they were when to their dismay they found that Jim had pulled their leg. He once told a few lads that the preacher's apples were very good and that Mr Jenkins (my father's predecessor) had gone away on holiday. When the boys were climbing the apple tree the minister called out from the window and reprimanded them He told me of the time that Cardiff City won the cup in 1927 scoring the only goal. He demonstrated with some agility the way the goal was scored by suddenly shooting out his right foot. Then picking up a hammer he chuckled quietly adding that the Arsenal goalkeeper was a Welshman. I checked the story years later and indeed it was correct.

Before he started work, Jim would insist on reading the newspaper from cover to cover and in a sense became a source of information to the people who came to him. Many of these farmers had little time for reading, were without a newspaper and would gladly seek out Jim to receive the latest report about the war. He told one old boy that Hitler had set the Mediterranean on fire whilst another was told that the enemy

had now arrived in Builth whereupon the recipient picked up a pitchfork and shouted ,
"Let's go now and stop them."

One day JO discovered that the great Welsh boxer Jim Driscoll had died. Peerless Jim had been a gifted and talented Featherweight champion and a Welsh idol of the working classes.
"Any news today Jim?"
"I see that James Driscoll has passed away"
"Good God that is very sad"

The man had misheard Jim and thought the reference had been made to a certain James Rhosygog a well respected local farmer. The man went home feeling very sad and proceeded to put on his best suit, a bowler hat and rode to Rhosygog to offer his condolences. When riding across the farm yard the first person he saw was James himself.

Jim the Blacksmith spent many an hour with us as a family regaling us with his stories over a bite to eat, and there was always enough food to go around, and even spending as little time to play football with me in the field at the back of the house. He worked whenever he felt like it and would not be bossed about or placed under any pressure but it was such a privilege to have seen him at work: a master craftsman. He donated the hay from a little field he had at the back of the shop so that our goats could be fed and he pinched a swede from Tyrosser field saying to me with a wide grin on his face.
" Don't tell your father but old Dai's got plenty he won't miss one."

It's sad to see the old building an empty shell and sadder to see Beulah school desolate, the roof leaking and the walls crumbling. Whenever I pass I stop for a little while and listen to the echoing silence hearing in my own mind the ghosts of yesteryear laughing and singing and my heart is made lighter by the very fact that although I have few if any photographs of these people I am immediately transported back to those happy days.

The King was on his deathbed and the news wasn't very optimistic. I expect it was George V it was long before my time.

"How is the King today Jim..any news?"

"It says here. 'Yesterday he was holding his own..today I expect someone else is holding it for him"

****

Chapter Nine
The Four Seasons

My mother loved the Spring. It was without doubt her favourite time of the year when the earth took a deep breath and extended its new lease of life, the days started to lengthen and the air was full of the sweet sounds of singing birds. She always had a sense of expectation and optimism at this time of the year and when she would suddenly announce it was time for Spring cleaning it was the cue to exit stage left as quickly as possible. The cat would hurtle out the back door and venture into the jungle of the garden in search of new prey and excitement. I would find a ball and kick the hell out of it against the creaking garage door whilst my mother would, in a matter of moments, assume the guise of a Mrs Mop straight out of the Ealing studios but without the mock cockney accent and minus the drooping cigarette. Her sleeves rolled up and tucked beneath the arms of her pinafore, a turban towel around her head and armed with a bucket, a mop, a brush and duster she would attack the kitchen cum living room with a gusto. The chairs were placed on the table, the mats removed and given a good hiding outside the back door leaving clouds of dust everywhere scattering the chickens and creating a fusillade of noise as the mats smacked against the outside wall. Everything was washed or polished, scrubbed and dusted, licked and flicked at until at last it was completed and we returned to normal. Within hours all was as it had been before with newspapers still protruding from beneath the cushions, the oak table still standing like a colossus in the centre of the room and the cat lying peacefully near the grate dreaming of fat brown mice and clotted cream as the old clock stood ticking the time away.

The weather was always a focus of attention in the neighbourhood and became the usual topic of animated conversation. Most farms had a barometer hanging discreetly in the shadows of the hall, which when tapped gently with fingers would signify any imminent change in the weather. Would the mercury rise or fall and to which direction would the arrow point? Those fortunate to own a wireless would listen avidly to the well modulated vowels of the announcer proclaiming the weather forecast and amend their plans accordingly. If you could see the summit of a particular hill it was surely a sign of rain. And quite naturally when you couldn't make out its contours, it was raining. I often would profess loudly in the company of others.

"I think it's going to snow."

"No, no. The wind is in the wrong place." would come a sagacious reply which not only left me with a sense of failure at being totally wrong in my surmise but also a feeling of utter bewilderment as to the whereabouts of the wind. More often than not they were correct in their assumptions. I was told if you observed the cows in the field lying down it was a sign of rain or if the swallows swooped low along the river it was also a warning that rain was on its way. It rained a lot in Wales.

The first indications of Spring were exciting. Who would be the first to spot the sudden splash of colour when a snowdrop emerged from the hedgerows, soon to be followed by a motley collection of yellow daffodils? Gareth, my brother had heard from someone that there was a remote and strange place along a river side where daffodils grew wild in abundance and these would be ideal to collect as a present for my mother. He decided one morning to go in search of these wild flowers and quite naturally I was to accompany him as a kind of Boy Friday. I must have been about six at the time and I only vaguely remember it. I was still at an age where I did nearly everything my brother demanded. There was a surge of excitement within me as it was seldom that my brother would share something with me and give up his time. His mind was made up and he was determined to achieve his goal and we set out on our trip but without telling my mother. We climbed up the Ciliau and crossed the Dulais river somewhere seemingly miles away, through undergrowth and small valleys where our chirpy voices echoed and re-echoed in the Spring silence. We then followed the river upstream somewhere below Rhosygog until we finally came across the remnants of an old building, a memory of a wall by a green patch of pasture and lo and behold a collection of golden daffodils growing along the river bank. It was a joyous sight for me for now I knew we would soon start returning homewards for I was thirsty and wanted something to eat. My brother soon collected a bunch and pointed out the traces of the house walls. I began to wonder in my innocence who had lived here and had they too collected flowers or perhaps they had been too busy trying to survive in harsh conditions to worry about such trivial matters.

We returned slowly and deliberately like two explorers from a dark and untamed land. My brother offered his hand now and again if only to cross a stream or avoid sinking into the foul smelling and oily mud. Had we lost our way? It had seemed like hours since I had seen something remotely familiar and I suddenly began to ache for the comforts of my home. My brother was undeterred and we pushed on climbing, sliding, clambering and scuttling through hedges and thorns beneath branches of rotting trees squelching and stuttering until suddenly we were on the summit of the hill and below me was the familiar scene of our house and the river glistening in the pale sunshine with the field and surrounding trees. We began to run clutching the prized daffodils in our grubby hands streaming downwards through the dead ferns, the silver birches, the broken sharp grey flint stones, the red molehills until at last we hit the road leading to our house.

My mother was beside herself with worry and was standing outside on the bridge striding up and down in a terrible state of agitation. It was well after two o clock in the afternoon and we had left the house around ten. Her eyes were wild and wet and filled with a picture that I had not seen before. She berated my brother and shook me hard as I tried to smile and offer my bedraggled sympathy bouquet. Her anger eventually subsided, turning to relief and although she threatened to punish us, nothing came of it and soon we were seated around the table eating copious amounts of bread and butter, home made welsh cakes, fried bacon and chips whilst the daffodils lay in an untidy tangle in a jam jar on the mantelpiece.

As the days lengthened and the air became warmer I could hear the crying of the new born lambs in the surrounding fields, our old friends the birds returned, the dipper built its nest beneath the bridge and we knew soon that the swallows would pay us a visit. Catkins grew in the hedges above the pretty primrose, the forget-me-not the shy violet and the menacing foxglove, promising an abundance of hazel nuts. The hips and sloes began to emerge and the honeysuckle emitted its beautiful spring aroma through my bedroom window and the grass grew green again. The fields were ploughed and the seed planted and somewhere in the secret distance we heard the first song of the cuckoo and the mournful but long awaited melodious uttering of the curlew.

My knowledge of farming is very meagre and it is only memory that serves me well. I know that in those days that Spring time was the time for sowing and planting and as David lived on the farm I had no option but to be involved in farm life even only perhaps to serve as a gate opener or to collect stones in a bucket to prepare a field for ploughing. I would always enjoy helping out and to be thanked for my contributions clumsy and inept as they may have been. David's father was an accomplished ploughman and before settling at Penrhiwmoch had earned his living in this way. These were the days before the tractor and to see the skill and dexterity as he worked was an eye opener. Bending his back as he controlled the two horses the plough share gleaming in the light, he would cut a swathe through the red Breconshire earth. I marvelled at the way he managed to keep a straight line concentrating and uttering orders to the two horses raising his voice now and again to drown out the sounds of the crows which followed in his wake. He was also a wonderful hedger as he cut and spliced the young saplings bending and twining them so as when they grew the hedge would become strong, thick and symmetrical. This is now a skill of the past and seldom can one glimpse a beautifully cut hedge done in the tradition of the old farming ways. I see him now crouched over his work with the strong leather gloves that covered his hands up to the elbow brandishing a billhook curved and pointed and smiling as always, happy and contented in his work.

Spring grew and we celebrated Easter time with flowers now in abundance. Good Friday was quite a religious day then and my father preached his sermon on the passion of Jesus. I always found it a sad story and had great sympathy for those who could not prevent the gruesome scenario enfold. I pitied Judas and had sympathy also for Pilate who washed his hands of the whole thing and I could never understand, as a boy, why Christ would surrender to these people and not save himself. We children had to wear our Sunday best on Good Friday and behave accordingly whilst my mother would draw the blinds in the afternoon as a mark of respect for our Lord and we had jelly with bread and butter for tea.

Suddenly it was early summer, June was in her glory and it was shearing time on the farms. This was an important date in the country calendar and people helped each other, giving their labour freely in exchange for a return of the favour on another day. As I was the local minister's son I was often invited to these occasions and no matter how early I arrived the men were always at work. The labour would begin at first light and I remember vividly the sight of two rows of men on benches sitting opposite one another wearing denim overalls, collarless white shirts with a sheep nestling in the armchair of their thighs, working, cutting by hand with a pair of shears the fleece of a trussed sheep. They would work continually stopping occasionally for a glass of cider, calling out for "string" with which to tie the hind legs of the sheep, and to take a break to eat the delicious and constant supply of food in the farm parlour. The men would swop stories as they worked, recalling past memories, or they exchanged cigarettes or perhaps sang a well known song or familiar hymn tune. The talk was never dirty or bawdy but the banter was good natured, warm and with an immense sense of comradeship and solidarity. I knew then at an early age that these were my people with whom I had a great bond, a bond that would never be broken. The ages of the "sharers" as they were called, ranged from teenage farm servants to elderly veterans and my job on many an occasion was to supply the man who called out "string" with a piece of rough yellow stained cord. The sheep were first herded into a pen their fleeces overgrown and straggly then individually caught and dragged to the table for a haircut. It was a pleasure to see how a man could remove the whole fleece without causing the frightened animal any harm. The fleece was then immediately rolled up like a blanket and carted off to be laid on an ever growing pile in a warm dry place. The scalped animal was marked with pitch or a branding iron and let loose into an adjoining field looking forlorn and thin. The animal would bleat for a second or two and then in a moment would forget the whole ordeal and concentrate on nibbling the grass. When I was with Derek in Beulah or Dennis in Llanafan we would try to find out the proximity of the cider barrel and help ourselves to a little glass or two. The drink was cold, sweet, powerful and very intoxicating and would make you feel giddy or silly or both in a matter of minutes. I recall one time visiting three farms in one afternoon, drinking cider in all three places and floating and singing my way home serenading the trees and the sky feeling very happy indeed.

What I enjoyed most on these festive occasions was to be asked to go and have something to eat. This was an understatement in itself. I remember sitting at a huge table adorned with tureens of steaming vegetables and slices upon slices of beef, ham, chicken and pork the platter placed in front of me was covered with so much meat that I could not even recognise the willow pattern.

"Help yourself Dewi."

"Dig in preacher!"

"You must be hungry boy after all the work you've been doing."

These were the kindest words I ever heard and I caught hold alright stuffing myself silly in the process as the women of the house in their starched aprons looked on beaming happily. Then out to play for a while, hide and seek in the farm buildings, sliding down the hay ricks, or sitting on the fleeces being careful not to catch lice. In one farm they had an old three seater outside wooden toilet and we children would sit on it like three Roman soldiers and pretend to do our business laughing, giggling and producing outrageous and outlandish noises. Or perhaps we would witness the castrating of certain lambs and I knew nothing of what was really taking place but the farm boys didn't bat an eyelid. When the evening shadows drew longer and the work was all done the young men would organise a football match in one of the fields using their jackets as goal posts their cries and groans rising and falling in the darkening still night. I wanted to join in, but this game was strictly for grownups.

The summer seemed long, endless days of sun and shower and everlasting, carefree happiness. We would bathe in the river where the water always took your breath away and my brother constructed a raft nailing old planks of wood to empty oil drums and roping the whole thing together. We were a mixture of Swiss Family Robinson and a Celtic Robinson Crusoe. We had plenty of fun splashing around in the water steering the raft back over the pool where the trout darted into the darkness and our voices resonated beneath the bridge. Sometimes I would cut a hazel sapling from the hedge and sharpen the end so it represented a spear. I would hurl the weapon at the trout but never managed to pierce a fish or come close to catching it. The fish would spot my upraised hand and dart away to safer waters. Despite the ample opportunity, I never learned to swim, have an innate fear of the water and to this day I have an aversion towards the sea and swimming baths.

The weather was always unpredictable and fickle despite the barometer readings and the weather forecasts on the wireless. I think my maternal grandmother was very ill and my parents, along with my baby sister, went off one afternoon leaving my brother and I at home happy and contented. We had no inkling that perhaps the law was being broken and that we should not have been left alone. It was the time that nobody lived in the next door cottage. When the thrill of being unsupervised had begun to falter, I remember the day becoming quiet and sinister. The cat disappeared into the outbuilding its tail like an exclamation mark as the clouds grew in the sky. A few days earlier I had witnessed a strange grey bird gliding slowly up the river. In my vivid imagination it was a golden eagle but in reality it may have been a heron or even a stork. Now it was as if a blanket had been thrown over the land and the stillness was incredible. No birds sang and the silence grew in its intensity. I must have been around six years old at the time and all of a sudden I wanted to hear the dark brown sound of my father's voice or the fuss of my mother as she went about her business. My brother, assuming the role of the adult male, opened the front and back doors of the house as he sensed a storm was approaching. He had this notion that it was safer for the electricity to pass through the house without touching anything. My brother was always reading and would come out with facts like these. The sky was now a vague maroon in colour and the heat was increasing by the second. I remember going upstairs to my bedroom searching for a favourite toy but being drawn to the window and looking outside. The trees were almost indiscernible and the air hung still and silent, waiting. At last the silence was broken by an enormous clap of thunder, followed by others in rapid succession and a sudden flash of forked lightning. My brother came running in and we both tentatively looked out the window. The rain began to fall like needles and pins hammering the roof, window, the road and steam began to rise above the bridge. In a matter of minutes the river was yellow and overflowing as the rain hissed, the thunder boomed and the lightning flashed and flickered sending a series of silver messages across the sky. I began to think of all the wicked things I'd done and now God was about to punish me. But I was compelled to observe from the window the horror of it all as a cow suddenly appeared, wild and terrified, tail flashing as she crossed the river half swept away by the current struggling to rise out of the water and reach the field opposite the house. I swear that wild horses with silver hooves were drumming across the sky. My brother had turned pale his glasses misty and we knew not what to do. The safest place for a child is the sanctuary of his bed. That is where we both went holding each other under the sheets whilst the battle continued to rage unabated outside. And then abruptly it stopped and we could hear the plaintive but optimistic song of a bird in tune with the gurgling, rushing torrent and the sound of a motor car. My parents had returned and my mother ran into the house holding my sister in her arms her smile lighting the gloom and a look of undeniable guilt on her face.

As a result of the sudden storm, many a tree had been brought down and swept away in the torrent along with my brother's raft and when the water receded there was debris everywhere the fields either side of the river streaked with brown but in no time at all the sun shone again and the air cooled, the cat reappeared and purred brushing my leg looking for food and quite naturally the birds sang in unison.

The river played an important part in our lives for one of my dear father's few pursuits was his love of trout fishing. This was a very basic and unsophisticated hobby. His rod was home made, fashioned from dark wood, thin layers of hazel and stapled together with bands of copper. I was not interested in fishing but I was his companion whenever we ventured out together on a fishing trip. He would know the right time to go when the water in the river had changed colour and that a flood was on its way. He wanted the colour of the water to look like tea without milk the way my mother drank it. I think he enjoyed it more than I did. He would dress in an old coat and hat and look like some down and out that I had seen on a Swansea street. My mother, always conscious of his role as pastor, would pretend to be disgusted with his appearance and hoped nobody would see him and as the rain beat down out we would go. We never ventured very far but as the dusk turned to night it was a wonder to be by the river and enjoy its thrills and mysteries. He would crouch on the bank casting his rod into the dark water and be concentrating like an Indian scout or a safe cracker whilst I entered my own private world of cowboys or smugglers. Then look out! A sudden flash of white and a little fish would dance in the pale light. Grinning like a schoolboy he would deftly haul it in and with one sudden twist of his fingers end the fish's gasping. Then he would reach into his old tobacco tin which stunk when opened to reveal a melee of writhing worms and maggots. Then the procedure would be repeated as we gradually made our way down the river's edge where in some places the froth bubbled like beer and the mud was oily, sulphurous and crossing a hedge or two, bending under barbed wire in the process. I knew every inch of the area having explored it time and time again in my childish wanderings.

Although he tried once or twice to initiate me into the ancient art of fishing I wasn't really interested, more concerned with the marauding Comanche below Lletyerefail or the press ganged striped -sweatered stevedores that lay in wait around the next bend in the river. But I loved being in his company to watch him relax, to observe the way in which he smoked his cigarette, the manner in which he cast his rod his brow lined in concentration and the simple joy on his face when he caught a little trout. He pointed out, in day time, the names of birds that flew: a yellow hammer here, a willow warbler there and perhaps, if we got a glimpse of one, a lesser spotted woodpecker. Once, he had an implausible idea of trying to converse with a bird! I am not sure to this day whether he was serious or whether his tongue was firmly in his cheek. He had read in a book that if you hit two stones together making a noise it would attract a bird called a stone chat. I was ordered to strike two pebbles together on the riverbank one late afternoon in summer whilst he waited and waited for the reply...which sadly never came.

The fishing trip would end when I complained that the rain was running down by back and I was beginning to feel cold. Back to the house where my mother would gut and clean the little fish and we would all sit at the table and dutifully tuck in after she had fried them on the open fire in a little pan that sizzled and spat. I am not a lover of fish and I sensed I could taste the river in the white flesh of the little brown trout but my father was proud of his achievements and we never dreamed of spoiling his moment.

The countryside so memorably evoked in Hardy's writings and Constable's paintings was readily available to me as a child and to experience the changing of the seasons with all its mystery and subtlety was a privilege. Father would bring out the old scythe which I was not allowed to touch, and with his collar removed, sleeves rolled up revealing his arms with sinews like pieces of cord, he would cut the grass in the field behind the house. Oh the sweet smell of newly cut rich green grass which was the early signs of summer and then the change of scent as the grass turned to hay as it dried out in the sun. We had our own miniature hay making sessions to feed our beloved Nancy and Heather, which did not compare with the farmers'. Here I would lend a hand to anyone who was hay making in the neighbourhood with the possibility of a silver coin pressed into your hand or more probably a free meal. Haymaking was all done manually in those days and I would help by either pitching or standing haphazardly on the gambo settling the hay and ensuring it was evenly balanced. This was very exciting! Hold on tightly as the horse staggered towards the barn and the wagon rolled and trundled on its dried mudded, rutted track. I would lie on my back in a bed of sweet smelling hay with sometimes a few uninvited thistles seeing only the blue endless skies above with touches of cotton wool clouds trailing across the canopy. Then into the barn with its own mixture of intoxicating odours and shadowy smells where the hay was scattered and stacked up to the ceiling where the cobwebs glistened on the grey stone walls and sparkled in the honey coloured penetrating light.

The farmers had indeed to make hay whilst the sun shone and once in Brynmoelddu we all worked until past dusk in order to complete the job before the threatening rain of the morrow. As the clouds neared we worked harder and faster, the sweat running into my eyes and down the small of my back. It was night time with a purple sunset. There we all stood silhouetted against the sky as the big yellow moon rose over the distant hills and Pam had to hold a large torch shining it upwards as if trying to spot an enemy plane as the final field was completed and supper awaited us in the parlour to our great satisfaction. We were treated to hot steaming scotch eggs with tomato, ham, cheese and bread and butter, followed by apple tart, Welsh cakes and a jug of home made lemonade. An inspiration it was to merely to sit at the table, scrubbed and burned by the sun, in tune to the melody of happy and animated conversation with the satisfaction of knowing that a job had been well done.

Mid Wales is now predominantly a sheep farming area in terms of agriculture and post war changes in politics and economic growth have altered the way of life in many ways in the vicinity. Some of the old traditions have all but died out but in my childhood, farmers earned their living off the land and one of the most important aspects was not only hay making but also the harvest. Not so many farmers now grow and reap the corn and barley that was so popular in my salad days. It was hard physical work done by tough guys who cut and tied the sheaves by hand. There was no combined harvester in those days and my job whenever I helped, willingly and with great enthusiasm, was to "stook" the sheaves following in the wake of the men and creating a line of miniature Red Indian wigwams. It was very hard work and the corn was rough and tore your skin easily leaving marks and weals at the end of a long day. A similar process of hauling the stooks whenever they were ready for harvesting took place. Again the cart was heaped as high as possible and then the barns were full to bursting and the fields left desolate with a collection of circling birds and a haze of gold and yellow intermingling with the streaking rays of the setting sun. My hands were caked with yellow, the palms as smooth as pebbles and wrists and lower arms cut and streaked as a reminder of my toil. Oh the golden sunsets of childhood preserved within my memory and the voices that rise and fall for ever in an eternal journey.

The chapel would arrange for its Harvest Festival when the interior would be adorned with produce. The window sills were lined with cabbage, swede, carrot and potato. Flowers and fruit lay on the communion table and I was allowed to sit with my pals in the back pew. Here we would sit, David, Dennis and Tony and myself eyeing the girls whose apple cheeks and sun kissed hair of barley and corn complemented the occasion. Sometimes the Pentrebach boys would join us and we would sit solemnly in feigned innocence whilst Glyn made us laugh with his mischief and nonsense. Such services were always well attended as the people gave thanks for their produce. Each and every family was usually represented and father would preach on the sower and the seed and God's bountiful love and I loved to sing the two well known hymns, the words of which I knew by heart: "Come ye thankful people come" and the rousing "We plough the fields and scatter." The congregation took this hymn to their hearts and I never tired of hearing its refrain and to witness the joy on people's faces as they sang together as one. The Harvest festival was also a sign that summer was coming to an end and the days were shortening rapidly. The leaves on the old oaks were changing colour as the green turned to brown and purple and yellow. The sun's rays were getting weaker and it was time to put on a woollen jumper or wear a scarf as the wind rose.

After being back at school for a few weeks it was time once again to enjoy a familiar if short lived recreation.

"Iddlyack...my first crack!"

"Iddlyonker my first conker!"

The horse chestnut tree did not grow in the fields of David's farm or in my close proximity but there were two or three down at Penycrug. On a Saturday, when we had more time, Tony and I would go visiting Mrs Price and be sure to knock on her door to ask permission first. Mrs Price was always willing, was rather shy and said very little. Tony was an expert tree climber and in an hour or so we managed to haul ourselves a wonderful cache. The conkers lay in a sack, like prized jewels with a most beautiful sheen that looked like the colour of race horses and had the faint smell of vinegar. We took them home and divided our spoils. My "best" I would coat with vinegar and place them by the fire so their skins would harden ready for the competition that would take place in school. On the Monday as soon as playtime came, out would come the contestants swinging and cracking at the hanging targets. Some of the farm boys would get over excited their leather lace that strung the conker cutting your wrist or rapping your knuckles with such a force that the pain stayed with you for hours later. Sometimes the conkers would get entangled and the shouts of "string" were yelled in order to get an extra shot. Yet within a few days when the novelty had worn off and the lovely hue of their skin had darkened, the conkers became a memory until the next year.

As the season grew the leaves began to fall and when the first signs of frost appeared the leaves cascaded like confetti embellishing the footpaths that intertwined through the woods. The nights grew darker as soon as the clocks changed and Christmas seemed an eternity away. In the meantime November was a reasonable month in my calendar when the fair came to the Groe in Builth, Guy Fawkes night was celebrated and as a taster for Christmas, my birthday.

The fair was very exciting for me and I looked forward to it with much anticipation. The whole family had decided to visit the old town for the afternoon and I was to spend an hour or so at the Fun Fair spending the few shillings that I had saved for the occasion. On the morning of this particular day I practised my throwing skills down by the river aiming at a set of tin cans which had been strategically positioned to represent the coconut shy. I had so wanted to win a coconut and carry it around as my trophy. So the practice was very keen with able assistance from Dennis who offered advice re the positioning of the arm and the balance of my feet!

After a nice dinner we all travelled in the car to Builth and off I went to meet my pals who had already travelled there on the bus. The fair was noisy and brash as always with a mixture of side shows as well as amusements. I recall seeing an act where a conjurer dressed in a turban, his face brown from make up, pretended to swallow swords and proceeded to cut a young woman in half. He then produced "blood" on his hands and one young man from the audience shouted out.
"It's red ink not blood!"

This caused some commotion but the performer rode the retort, his eyes blazing and the sweat breaking out on his forehead lining his made up face and got through his act. I saw pictures of a bearded lady, a dwarf and a child with two heads, I rode the Ghost Train which was quite scary and managed to drive a bumper car where the young male attendants with greased hair and perpetual cigarettes, tattooed and ringed tried to seduce the girls as they swayed and sauntered, riding the rodeo of the dodgem cars collecting the fares, their hands as black as colliers. There was some show where a scantily dressed young lady stood outside, rather self consciously on a raised platform but for reasons known only to adults I was not permitted to enter. And all the time the lights blazed, the lilting soundtracks of songs were heard dipping and rising in the stiff wind amidst the shrieks and screams and the whole scene burst with a colourful clamour. I tried to win a goldfish by throwing a ping pong ball into a bowl which always missed and left me with a sense of increasing frustration as the bored and impassive teller took my damp pennies without a grunt. Similarly I would try to pierce the Ace card with a set of darts that went everywhere except the target. Then to eat a disgusting toffee apple on a stick which was syrupy and dirty and tasted like cod liver oil. My favourite was the simple game of Rolling Pennies where the odds against your winning anything remotely profitable were scandalous. The coin always seemed to lodge itself just the wrong side of the line so your long awaited win was always out of sight.

As the afternoon proceeded I kept waiting to build up enough confidence to try to win a coconut holding a sixpenny piece in my hand. Dennis and I had looked around enough and now I was ready and I knew the farm girls would be easily impressed if I won the prize. At last I mustered up enough pluck and stepped forward. Three wooden balls for sixpence and six battered tins to knock to the ground. Nobody was watching except Dennis, as I took aim. Crash! and the first ball dislodged the target sending three tins to the sawdusted floor. Bang! and the second ball sent two more tins to the ground. Now one ball left and one tin standing there like a crooked shadow. I breathed in and narrowed my eyes and took careful aim. Wallop! I hit the target full on sending it hurtling upwards as the wooden missile thudded unto the sacking behind. The attendant nodded briefly without a glimmer of a smile as I stepped forward and selected a large coconut remembering to shake it near my ear as I had seen others do. I was a conquering hero and I strutted around the fairground until it was time to go home with my prized possession held in the palm of my hand. I heard a female voice calling.

"Oh Dewi Glandulas have won himself a coconut. Well done him then."

My parents were not duly impressed, my sister had had a ride on a roundabout, my brother had bought himself a magazine about mechanical engineering and when the coconut was cracked open, the juice was sour, the flesh barely edible and the shells were later used to carry grain to the chickens and to imitate the sounds of galloping hooves by the Winter fireside. The pursuing posse soon faded into the sinking sunset.

My father came home one day from a visit to Builth or perhaps it was Brecon carrying a wrapped parcel under his arm, It was a box of fireworks in preparation for bonfire night or as Tony called it "Dai Fox night". We were allowed to place each firework on the table careful not to go too near the fire and to inspect the goods with care. There was a Roman Candle, a Squib, a Banger, a Jackie Jumper which was in effect really a loose cannon, a Catherine Wheel, a Vesuvius, a Mighty Atom and a Rocket together with a packet of sparklers and a motley collection of others whose names are lost to me. My father would then take charge of the whole box which would not reappear until the actual night. I knew he had secreted them in a drawer in his desk nestled against his prized ostrich egg and an unplayable ocarina.

Preparation would commence for the big night. I would collect wood and dead ferns from the fields around us and these were deposited in a suitable safe spot in eager readiness. Cardboard boxes and newspapers and anything that was expendable were thrown on to the increasingly growing pile. The Brecon and Radnor joined forces with The Western Mail and amalgamated with The Lion and The Eagle comics. Then to make the Guy: one of my father's old trousers was stuffed with newspaper, the legs tied at the bottom and an old sack was stuffed with similar cast-offs and stuck on to a piece of wood so that it looked something like an effigy. Then a hat of any shape was added and then he was despatched to the condemned cell of the unguarded coal shed to await his execution.

Our special guest for the evening was none other than Mr John Williams the Villa known to all as Johnny Villa which in retrospect sounds like the name of a notorious Mexican revolutionary or a back street bantam weight boxer. Johnny took his role very seriously and as a bachelor probably enjoyed himself as well in the company of children. Johnny would come down in the late afternoon wheeling a wooden wheelbarrow laden with old wood and out of date copies of The Farmer's Weekly for the bonfire. He also had a small bottle of paraffin, a box of matches and an old fashioned lantern inside which was a small candle. It was Johnny who would light the bonfire ensuring that we children stood at a safe distance from the blaze. I would try to bake a potato in the fire but later when I tried to eat it, it was either as hard as a stone or burnt through leaving me with a mouthful of ash. Johnny would crouch over the fire adding a little paraffin whenever necessary and we tried not to laugh as his grey trilby was perched back to front on his bald head.

And then the fireworks would start when my father was totally in charge. First of all we were all given a sparkler and when ignited would flare up with a bright white light and throwing sparks everywhere which would illuminate our faces half hidden in shadow. I did not like the noise of the bangers but marvelled at the soft, beautifully smelling pretty ones that resembled a flowing river on fire or a small multi- coloured volcano. Then the Catherine Wheel which sometimes needed a kick start as it suddenly revolved, nailed to a post, whirling in a rapid melee of mayhem. At last the rocket! How far would it go? Would the family of Tyrosser discover it lodged in a tree? Would it go down our chimney? Placed in an open bottle neck my father would ensure our safety and then light the fuse. The sky was filled with a million stars of many colours lighting up the sky with a brief blitz of a promise and then darkness. We tried to keep the fire going but soon it was a cluster of shadows around a smoking ember the sudden gust of wind showering the area with sparks and my sister retired to bed, the adults went in for supper and my brother and I poked the last remains of the blaze with a long stick and I felt sad that the guy was gone for another year, but not to worry, my birthday was just around the corner.

Celebrating my birthday was never a lavish affair and there certainly wasn't the apparent obsession that seems to be today for greetings cards. I certainly got one from my parents and often one from my mother's two sisters. I sometimes received a postal order for five shillings which would be cashed the next time I ventured into Builth. I usually received a small present in the shape of a book and I had a little party with the usual crew on a Sunday afternoon. We played games and sang around the piano as my mother played with some dexterity from the rusty red coloured book called The National Songbook containing melodies from all the home nations and which was kept in the piano stool whose hinges were loose and when you sat on it to play at the piano your backside would shift one way and then the other. We sang Tavern in the Town, The Ash Grove and Little Brown Jug. Tony had a quiet reedy voice barely in tune, David on the other hand was born to sing but poor old Dennis was totally out of tune. My brother usually vacated the room and went elsewhere to read and took very little notice of us. We had tinned fruit with ideal milk which I could not tolerate, cakes and perhaps a jam sponge. One year I received a card with a red badge with white printing saying "I am 9 today" which I could only wear for a day on my lapel but I kept in my drawer for a lot longer. David's mother was always very kind and would invariably knit me a pair of gloves which were very useful as the cold weather was just around the corner.

The snow would come every year without fail and without warning, stealthily sneaking up at night so when the morning came there was a hush upon a silence and the world looked like ice cream with a scattering of Christmas trees. Even the river's song was subdued and many a time the water would be frozen over when the hard frost bit in. This meant that the roads would be impassable for a few days, the school bus would not come so my brother would not go to the county and the school car would not attempt to scale the pitches of Brynmoelddu and Tyrosser. My sister would be too young to attempt the trek which meant that I could undertake one of my great adventures: Walking to school in the snow.

Standing by the window of my little bedroom and surveying the scene was like looking at a giant Christmas card in all its magic and all its romance. There was no sign of life anywhere and the sky was so low that you could barely recognise the line drawn between the earth and the heavens. My mother sensed my excitement and would ensure that an extra woollen garment would lie beneath my navy gabardine coat and that a rough coarse balaclava was the order of the day. I was reluctant to wear this but glad of it a few minutes later when the wind's icy tentacles would embrace you. Breakfast of "shink" and a fried egg with buttered bread and off I'd go out the back door trudging through the already drifted snow and out on the road. There was not a trace of a wheel print and I bent my head to the hill and proceeded. Half way up by the old oak tree I would wave to my mother as she was standing in the kitchen waving a white cloth back at me.

Tyrosser was as quiet as a cathedral. A dog came out and sniffed at me and head held low, turned in disgust, pretending to be a wolf, heading back to the warmth of the barn. There was a sign of footprints but no sound. On across the straight to the Llwyngwrgan turning when again there was no trace of other people. Was I the only one alive in the world for the hushed silence hung heavy on the air with perhaps the murmur of the wind? Here I was, Scott of the Welsh Antarctic trudging onwards gallantly for the Empire or was I a trapper in the Yukon. The duck farm was silent and not a quack was heard, the pond half frozen in the dim light and only a glimpse of a faint glow from Penywaun window. Now I was running kicking up the snow like a cowboy on his horse, down Brynmoelddu pitch to meet the traces of those who had gone before me. I recognised the wellington prints in the snow and counted three pairs of footprints. This could only mean Gareth and Dawn from Trefan and Pam. My heart skipped a beat. Would I catch them up before school or would the Dolfan boys meet them before I did? Somebody had made the mark of a giant bird's footprints in the snow, and here was a message for me which read.

"Catch us up if you can"

When I got to Dolfan there was smoke rising from the chimney, the blue a striking contrast to the silver and white of the morning and I could hear the faint sound of the cattle being fed. I caught a glimpse of Gomer standing tall and broad framed within the cowshed door. He did not see me. Too busy and too preoccupied with his work. Back on the road following in the wake of the ghosts ahead of me. I was alone again and loved the sense of the solitary also knowing that school was now only a few hundred yards away.

It was as if I were walking in a dream on a cold frozen landscape where nobody spoke and all noises were hushed seeing people who could not see me. An observer in my own life.

The journey back from school was quite different. Because of the inclement weather, we were allowed to go home early before the darkness came and before the frost made serious damage to the snows. We would travel together, we children. laughing and playing, sliding and skidding, making snowmen on the way and hurling snowballs at all and sundry. At the bottom of the hill we would part and I was alone again with the prospect of ploughing my way home. Then the frost would start and in a matter of seconds the knuckles on my fingers would change colour as the frost embraced your whole body in its mighty grip. Wrap the scarf around you and push on as the shadows deepened and the contours of the land changed abruptly. One or two cars had passed this way earlier and now the wheel marks were frozen over and black in colour as a vivid contrast to the white. I could feel my wellington tops cutting into my legs and the soreness growing with the minute. And then the glow of the window of my house and its warmth awaited me. I ran down the hill sliding and shouting at the same time hearing only my own shrill and piping voice and in a matter of minutes I'd be at the fire side a book in hand my coat steaming in the corner, my hands aching with the return of the warmth, my feet numb and my sisters cheeks red and glowing like the whistling wood on the fire.

The drifts were dangerous. When the wind changed direction and blew strongly the back door of the house would be covered and the drifts would rise almost to the roof. When outside we would explore the depth and sometimes one could be almost buried.Then when the snow had settled and the frost had made natural slides and ski slopes I would "borrow" my mother's enamel bowl and sitting in it like some Buddha would slide down the slope in the field the seat of my trousers soaked through. My mother pretended once again to be cross, but allowed Hefina to sit on my lap as we both hurtled and spiralled down the incline. Simple pleasures were compounded when Gareth created a sledge from an old piece of zinc turned and hammered in the front to produce a kind of wind break and a piece of rope was inserted through two punctured holes and hey presto even Father Christmas would have been impressed. We would watch out for the mail van with its bright red colour a blaze and my mother would insist I present the driver with a hot steaming cup of tea. We would look closely to see if the wheels of his van were supported by chains. If this was so we knew that the snow was serious.

When the thaw came the snow would shift off the roof of the house sliding down to the ground like a mini avalanche and I knew then that the snow would soon be another memory. The grass would reappear as the snow changed colour turning to muddy slush and when the snow disappeared the land looked refreshed and the fields very green indeed. I wasn't too upset to see it go although I had loved running through its depths and also marking out the field as a football pitch. I had not enjoyed the chilblains or "giblins" as they were known, and I had endured the pain and discomfort of earache. My mother's remedy for this was for me to go to bed at night with a hot sock filled with salt pressed to the aching ear. It usually worked. but only in time.

Sometimes the snow came before Christmas and sometimes afterwards, but Christmas itself was always a permanent fixture and for all children past and present it was a joyous time. My brother of course had dismissed the whole concept of Santa Claus or "Sion Corn" as a blatant act of fiction and a lot of nonsense. On the other hand my baby sister believed it all and I for one was not going to shatter her illusions. Gareth would, when it occurred to him, have a quick search through my father's study and once came across a box of paints which ended up in my stocking. I was happy to await whatever I was given and although we received very little I cherished them and to this day I still have my long bow, minus the arrows, my Hornby train set, my Subbuteo Football game and half a dozen books which, when opened, unleash a festoon of memories.

We never had a turkey, settling for a plump chicken with roast potatoes, sprouts and a variety of vegetables. Mother would make a Christmas pudding with a white sauce and we had to eat it carefully because of the hidden silver threepenny bits that were contained somewhere in the morass. We had furnished the house with a few coloured decorations, a collection of balloons and a red nosed cut out of Father Christmas that came out every year to groans and protests and had a smile reminiscent of Jim Matthias.

One Christmas Eve my sister was allowed to share my bed and to participate with me in that solemn of all solemnities: opening the stocking on Christmas morning. We went to bed quite early with our torches ready for the morning but we couldn't sleep. I told her stories of how Santa had such a lot of work to do; his reindeer were hungry and so on until she finally went to sleep. And then to awake in the still, early, hours of the dawn where nothing stirred only the beating of our hearts.

"Has he been yet?"

"I'm not sure..let's go and see..shhh..don't wake anybody."

We shone our torches onto the wall of the room creating an instant cartoon character and slowly crept out of the bed. The floor was icy cold and a board creaked in the cold breath of the special morning. Down the stairs we crept like two cat burglars whispering in our conspiracy, her tiny hand clutched in mine. In the gloom of the kitchen where the white ashes of the long gone wood fire spilled on to the grate, I could see a stocking for each of us children. My brother, despite his protestations, would gladly accept any gift so he was certainly not left out. There was a parcel each and we collected them our breath trailing like smoke.

"Look, a note from Santa"

"Read it to me."

It was written in Welsh with my father's unmistakable handwriting from his fountain pen although he had pretended to be cold and it was shaky.

"Thank you for the mince pie. Love Santa"

We carried our swag back to the warmer climes of the bed and with eager excitement that we could hardly contain, opened our presents. The woollen stockings appeared to have a series of disjointed knee caps as an orange and then a tangerine was retrieved, Once there was a horse on a plastic stand that bucked and kicked when pressed and a kaleidoscope where a series of never ending patterns was produced, a metal frog which made a funny noise which irritated everyone in turn, a painting book, a box of crayons and a whole assortment of cheap but beautiful treasures. I was always grateful for anything I was given remembering that other children would be lucky to get an orange, a handkerchief and a pair of gloves. The rest of the afternoon was spent playing with our new presents, eating until I felt sick and counting the stars above the wood when the magical night descended. My father came in from getting more wood for the fire and I heard him say to my mother, his face soft and almost child like.

"Do you know, I swear the wind was humming Silent Night outside tonight"

On Boxing Day the Villa family would come for tea. This was Johnny and his two spinster sisters. They were lovely, simple, clean living God fearing innocents, kind, gracious, well mannered and generous. My mother would light the fire in the front room which resulted in smoke filling the chamber until it caught properly and with no ventilation, the walls would eventually stream with condensation. The sisters were always interested in what went on and once Catherine praised my attempts at landscape painting.

"Oh. That's lovely. It's very good indeed. What is it?"

Both Beulah chapel and Troedrhiwdalar chapel would have a Christmas party for the children in the area and I, naturally attended both. They were wonderfully exciting times and we each were given a small gift and an orange along with a party where we played all the usual games and sang carols around an old piano. Yes. We all sang the irreverent words to the carols like " whilst shepherds washed their socks by night" and "we three Kings of orient are one in a taxi two in a car" and thought we were very daring and bold. Then "Santa" would pay a visit complete with an ill fitting beard a spotless pair of wellingtons and a strong and usually recognisable Breconshire accent. Who would be the first to spot his true identity? Then in turn the child's name would be called out and he or she went up to receive the gift. Some younger children were afraid and would burst into tears seeing this rather grotesque stranger in a red coat sitting in a chair surrounded by laughing women. One year in Beulah it was Jim Matthias giving an award winning performance as Saint Nicholas and when I received my present I said.

"Thanks Jim"

"Alright boy." was his reply, eyes like meteors smiling through his mask.

And soon the New Year would arrive without a fuss, with little celebration and the Christmas decorations were rolled up and boxed away for another year, some cards used for painting and drawing on and we were into January and February where the cold had its grip. The river would perhaps freeze over again but nothing like the long bad winter of '47 where people walked on the hedges to get to the shops, and in time the first touch of Spring would re- appear and the whole miraculous, happy process would begin again. I began to sense a feeling of deep melancholy, a sense of impending doom almost, that I was a year older and that my childhood days, glorious and loving though they certainly were, would shortly be left behind for ever. But not just yet.

****

Chapter Ten
Coronation Year

Nineteen fifty three was Coronation year and I would guess I was as near to being at my childhood peak as Edmund Hilary was to his peak: Everest. It was indeed the year of Queen Elizabeth's coronation, the ascent of the highest mountain in the world, the year that saw the inimitable Stanley Matthews attain his coveted cup winner's medal at Wembley Stadium and Bryn and Miriam moved in next door.

The little cottage next door had been vacant for quite a while and in the meantime my brother and I had continued our cat burglary apprenticeship climbing in through the skylight and exploring every room that was there. So when Gomer Lewis called at the house once and asked my father about the cottage, I was able to secure an entrance by firstly ascending the roof via the washhouse and opening the door so that Gomer had an unofficial look around much to his amusement and my father's quiet smile. But, for whatever reason the Dolfan family did not move in as our new neighbours. I was a little disappointed at this not only as I admired Gomer and saw him as a John Wayne character but the three sons would have shared my passion for football and all things that veered to North by North West.

Bryn and Miriam Jones was a joyous couple who had recently married. Obviously much in love, they were now moving in next door as our close neighbours. I was delighted as Bryn was the younger brother of Dennis Brynmoelddu and was well known to me as the uncle of Pam, Ian and Colin. Bryn was young and handsome with jet black hair and twinkling eyes. He reminded me of Rock Hudson who was at that time an up and coming Film Star. He spoke quickly, the words pouring out of him in true staccato fashion and he laughed a lot his whole body shaking as he did so. He was physically very strong and worked at Brynmoelddu with his older brother. Nobody could throw a cricket ball as high into the sky as he could and he played a game of rings with me and I'm not sure whether he allowed me to win or not. They settled in very quickly and it was nice to hear other voices in the close proximity of my home.

Miriam was young and lovely looking, one of several sisters from the Powell family in the Llanafan area. Llanerchlwyd. She was full of high spirits, house proud, her voice full of laughter and she had an attractive singing voice. It was not long before she would be in the front room whilst my mother played the piano and Miriam sang. She was good company for my mother and they became close friends remaining so until my mother's death in old age. Most of the songs that echoed around the house were straight out of the Sankey or the Congregational Hymn Book but one or two others stay in my memory: "Count Your Blessings", "If I can help somebody" The German song translated as "The Happy Wanderer," and there was another called "Sweet Violets" which had a sad refrain and was sentimental to say the least. I have never heard that song since then. Of course "We'll keep a welcome" has become a classic in some ways although I now find it a little embarrassing to hear. Another popular song of that era was "Now is the Hour" which never fails to bring a lump to my throat especially if one of my mother's favourite singers sang it. Gracie Fields. But Bryn and Miriam were an item and were immediately loved by all of us.

That year the roadmen had been busy trimming the sides of the main road and cutting back the verges and generally having a nice time of it. They would come in the morning and work at their own chosen speed, their voices rising and falling in musical conversation and tobacco smoke drifting in the still air. A little later a man would come with a Steam Roller and sleep in a little wooden caravan by the crossing. I have vague memories of a man smoking a pipe and looking pensively out of the wooden door. I had been warned to stay away from the stranger and I did although a girl in Beulah had been offered half a crown to reveal a particular part of her body to someone there. All very strange and weird for a boy of ten.

Dennis and I decided then to build a dam for the summer and we set about it shoving and pushing big boulders from the river itself and collecting other stones and pieces of debris, planks of abandoned wood and empty boxes. It took a long time but eventually we managed to make a kind of crossing which was topped by the pieces of turf that the roadmen had cut and had discarded in the hedges. We had created our own swimming pool, a pleasant area for the brown trout, and were so successful at our engineering feat that Bryn was able to prance across the river as a short cut to feed the chickens in the henhouse in the field on the other side. I think he may have got his feet wet at times. The days were long and the skies eternally blue, or so it seemed. In November of that year, on the 27th which was my birthday, their first born child was born next door. I was terribly excited as Jimmy, their beautiful baby boy would now share my birthday. I recall being allowed upstairs to see the little baby lying on his mother's breast in the double bed and I was thrilled to bits. I had noticed a few weeks earlier that Miriam had slowed down a lot and when I asked my mother if Miriam was alright she said that she was suffering from a bad back. A few days after Jimmy was born I told my mother in no uncertain terms.

"Don't you go having a bad back Mama." That year Bryn planted a fir tree across the road near to the blacksmith's shop to commemorate the birth of his only son. The tree still grows tall and straight ascending heavenwards.

Mr D. I. Davies told us one morning in school that the highest mountain in the world had at last been climbed and we were to be proud that Britain had raised the Union Jack at its peak. He also added that Sherpa Tensing, who was not British, had also reached the summit but there was less fuss made of the Tiger. Sir John Hunt who was the leader of the expedition had lived in Knighton in Radnorshire but when I questioned my father about him he had very little to say and carried on reading or scribbling. Why were parents so closed in those halcyon days of the nineteen fifties? When I asked certain questions I did not always receive the appropriate answer. There was soon a picture of the ascent of Everest pasted on the classroom wall with the flag resplendent and the goggles askew and smiles everywhere. Later I think we saw a film in the school room where we watched in admiration the shaky crumbling footage accompanied by stirring incidental music.

The whole of the United Kingdom, known then as Great Britain, was preoccupied with the Coronation and in Beulah school we were all instructed to compile a scrapbook with cuttings and photographs of the new young queen. The Western Mail and the Cymro were the only newspapers we had along with the Brecon and Radnor Express so information was sparse to say the least. My parents showed very little enthusiasm for the whole thing but I was more excited about the sports and the celebrations consisting of a bonfire and real fireworks. On the other hand my father, in his official capacity as the pastor was on the committee to organise the celebrations. I still have a school exercise book with the minutes of each meeting impeccably recorded in my father's handwriting. I recognise nearly all of the names noted in the little book from the organisers to the names of the children involved. Every child was to receive a coronation mug as well as a tea party and sweets and every competitor in the sports, winner or loser, would receive an extra shilling. Donations from local people amounted to just over £82 which in those days was a substantial sum of money. What I find so touching when re- reading these minutes is the generosity of the people, their sense of solidarity and their warmth with each person making a contribution in some way or another: giving money, allowing the use of a field for the sports, organising the sporting events, donating food and the like. There was also a small grant from Breconshire Education Committee totalling £8 to be shared amongst every school child. My father had scribbled on the back of an envelope which I found within the pages of the exercise book, the names of all the children likely to be present at the event and I remember them all. Some are living and some are gone to other areas or have since died. The number of persons likely to attend was: adults 210, school children 59 and pre school children 36. A grand total of 305.I suppose it was like this all across the country, in tiny villages and small towns and I certainly enjoyed it. I enjoyed the sports, the jelly and the fireworks.

We had been invited as a family to watch the historic televised event up at a farm called Tynclun. There lived an Italian whom we called Mr Bell and his Swiss wife who sometimes came to the little services at Capel Rhos. He said very little. He was short swarthy and had black brylcreemed hair in waves. She, I think was well off, and wore real leather boots and a long overcoat. I recall that she was very glamorous in a toned down way and had three small daughters. The Bells must have had generated their own electricity as we all still relied on oil lamps and candles then and to be present in a farmhouse with electric light was a novelty. But this was June, a fine day as I recall and the room was in semi darkness to complement the little brown wooden Television set that flickered in the corner. There were many guests there that day and Mrs Bell was a very kind and generous hostess with copious cups of tea, cakes and sandwiches. I found the whole televised service rather tedious, the singing in the cathedral very loud but I was distracted by the sight of Pat Lewis in her running shorts in preparation for the forthcoming sports. I too had my shorts and daps ready and I couldn't wait for the real celebrations to begin. I remember seeing the young, newly crowned queen, radiant and rather beautiful if a little nervous as I expect I would have been with millions watching my every move.

I loved the sports. The smell of crushed damp green grass, the lorries selling fruit and vegetables, the taste of dark blue plums from a brown paper bag, the throngs of happy people winding in and out in eternally autumn colours and greys, a sepia coloured photograph. I recall the boys on heavy black bicycles, the sheep dogs trailing around sniffing everything in sight, sly eyed and sneering. There was noise and the hullabaloo, the snorting Welsh cobs and the miscellany of other events which took place; the animated laughter that emanated from the back door of the Red Lion and the secrecy of the shadowed forbidden interior with its enticing smells that both enthralled and disgusted.

I entered everything that day running, leaping, juggling, rolling and generally exhausting myself: the 100 yards, the 220, long jump, high jump, egg and spoon race, relay, three legged race and the sack race and by the end of the afternoon had amassed well over a pound in prize money clutching the clammy silver coins in my hands like some Welsh speaking Scrooge. We had all won something except for my brother who sullenly refused to partake in anything as foolish

and as immature as this. I remember Bill Jones
Oakfield winning a race running in his stockinged
feet, his crooked nose leading the way and he was
well over sixty years of age then. Uncomfortably
I remember a boy being lathered by his father,
strapping him with his belt because the boy had
"borrowed" a bike without permission and had
sneaked off with some older boys to the far away
town of Llandrindod. I remember acutely the
public humiliation and the sense of shame as the
onlookers watched in utter dismay, mouths open
but unwilling or afraid to interfere.

Later there were the five a side football
matches with the local farm boys forming their
own teams and the pillow fights where two men
contested one another trying to knock each
other's blocks off with heavy laden sacks
balancing astride a wooden stile construction. I
was half hoping my father would compete in this
but when I saw the look in his eyes when I
jokingly suggested it I shut up abruptly. The most
exciting event to close the show was the tug of
war but when Beulah faced Llanafan I could
support neither but watched in fascination at the
excitement of it all. Teams of eight face each
other and the rules are very simple. Try to pull
the opposition over a sawdust line. But
sometimes the event would last a long time with
both sides gaining advantage then allowing it to
slip away. It was fascinating to see grown men
demonstrating their strengths to the sounds of
"Take the strain.....heave..heave...dig in dig in!
Hold 'em boys..hold 'em." and the heels of their
hob nailed boots would cut up the grassy surface
leaving marks and bruises. There would be one
man at either end of the line who acted as the

linchpin and he would roar out the instructions. Red faced and jacketless the men would lie on the ground afterwards panting and making a show especially if the women were watching but all in good humour and all in good fun.

When the shadows began to lengthen the fireworks and bonfire display began and I was presented with a mug which I still have to this day although I fear it is now somewhere in the attic gathering dust along with so many of my other memories. Mr Swan was in charge I remember, stamping his military authority everywhere. My father did his bit in his usual modest and quiet way and as the night grew darker and the last rocket veered its way skywards searching for the stars and the dying embers of the wood bonfire crackled and spat we ambled our way home, families and groups of people walking, flashlights at the ready and a few cars revved their engine and a bike whooshed past in the dark. Happy and homeward bound with a pocket full of silver and an aching body I pondered with the idea on what I was going to spend my prize money.

Eight months prior to the coronation the newly uncrowned Queen came to visit us along with her husband Prince Philip. When I say this, she did not actually call at the house for a cup of tea with my mother whilst Dat and Philip discussed the growing of beetroot in the garden. Claerwen dam in the Elan Valley was to be officially opened by the Queen. Here was a new dam that had been built to provide further water for the people of Birmingham. The Elan valley is a wild romantic mountainous region of Radnorshire with connections with the poet

Shelley and a drowned village complete with a submerged church. When the royals arrived she was not only greeted by local dignitaries in their official capacity, but several local people from the Llanafan area rode on horseback up over the Dulas valley and over the top of another range. There is a snapshot somewhere of the riders waving and doffing their hats, silhouetted like guarding Comanche against a pale sky. Amongst the intrepid travellers were Elvet Oakfield, Gwladys the post woman, Ivor Tanrallt and Lil from Erwddol. The romance continues....

All the neighbouring schools had a part to play in the visit of the Queen. In my school we had been ordered to wear our best clothes and to be sure to wear a cap and then stand dutifully in line on the road near Newbridge on Wye to wave and remove as ordered, the wretched cap as she passed. How we got to Newbridge I do not remember but I do recall standing in the cold October day in my navy gabardine coat holding my little sister's hand along with what seemed hundreds of school children. When she appeared in her big black shiny car she waved at me, smiled and the Prince also nodded. It was all over in a flash but my sister began to cry because she had not seen her. Hefina had some notion of seeing a woman with a crown on her head straight out of the fairy stories. She was so upset that my father had to take us that evening in our own shiny black car to Llandrindod to watch the royal party depart on the royal train. I think the queen remembered me as the smart young lad with well combed hair who had so solemnly taken off his cap for her for she smiled at me again although Philip looked puzzled, detached and bored stiff and for some reason averted his gaze. Perhaps I had offended him. I picture my father standing outside the paper shop in his dark overcoat, his clerical collar as white as a swan, holding my sister in his arms and pointing the queen out to her. Nothing more was said about the whole adventure and my father was more interested in the shop window and the books on sale than the visiting establishment figures from England.

I went for a week's holiday to stay with my Aunty Enid and my grandparents at Craigcefnparc. But before I stayed there we visited Swansea and went into the large old fashioned indoor market there. The market has changed very little since the war, a large echoing place with fresh produce on display, fresh fish from the local sea and a black turd- like concoction called larva bread which is by and large a local seaweed speciality that my grandfather ate. The market has no order with a miscellany of goods on sale from novelty toys to patriotic red and white scarves and rugger shirts to shiny imitation miners lamps, the miners all have gone now, and in 1953 a handsome looking cricket bat hanging up to catch my eye for the price of eleven shillings and six pence. I looked lovingly at it and it had a spring in its handle which indicated to me that it was a real bat and no cheap imitation. I bought it on the spot and it became, for many years my prized possession. Other boys laughed and called it Williams's golden bat. Of course it was hardly more than a sophisticated toy but to me it was indeed the golden bat and further more, I had paid for it with my own money, money that I had earned honestly and justly. Later that year, I painted a black V on the bottom as I had seen a picture of Cyril Washbrook going out to bat with a splendid looking blade that resembled mine.

I had a wonderful time at my Grandfather's house which had been my father's boyhood home. I played a tuneless piece of music on the Harmonium in the front room, examined the two china cows on display and counted the home-made walking sticks hanging on the stairs rail. Sometimes I helped out in the cobbler's shop where my grandfather sat, surrounded by boots of all shapes and sizes, a black bucket in which he expertly spat his chewed tobacco juice and where the smell of leather and tobacco filled the room. But I was a hindrance to him, too young to discuss politics or theology or the basic rudiments of Welsh poetry. My maiden Aunt spoiled me rotten and as I was the only child there, I had everyone's attention. She did insist on scrubbing my ears holding me firmly by the scruff of the neck and the stink of carbolic soap filling the wash house outside. She was kindly and child- like in many ways always filling and sending off crossword puzzles and entering simple competitions in the eternal hope that one day she would win a prize. She never did. To add a sense of irony to the situation it was Derby Day and I was only just about interested but I did have a list of the runners in the newspaper and I jokingly asked my aunty who was busy preparing the dinner, who would win the race. She, in a hurry read the first name on the list. "Oh I haven't time now, quick oh alright! Pinza. He'll win it. When we had finished eating I asked permission to turn on the radio and when we heard the commentator saying that Pinza was taking it up inside the final furlong I couldn't believe it and of course Aunty Enid was totally bewildered.

"I wish I had put a shilling on it now." She gasped. I don't know what the odds were, but it was ridden by the great jockey Gordon Richards.

My pal, Byron Watts who lived about two hundred yards away, came to play and we enjoyed the cricket, with my new bat, and football down on a real football pitch with goals that had a cross bar. Here a few others joined in and we all got on quite well speaking Welsh and having a laugh. It was around that time that Byron and I went to the pictures in Clydach travelling on the bus the few miles to the small town. It was here that I saw The Quiet Man. It enthralled me so much, falling in love with Maureen O Hara and admiring the gentle John Wayne character who wore a blue ring on his right hand. It was set in county Mayo in the west of Ireland but it might just as well have been filmed in North Breconshire because the characters were easily identifiable and the story familiar, simplistic and non-threatening. Years later I was to acquire a copy of the film on video and even visit the area where the film was shot but nothing could beat the first time I set eyes on it. I was captivated by the sentimental love songs and the gentle humour that filled the little cinema. When I came out into the drab little street with the traffic and the smoke from the nickel works near by, I felt homesick for my home and all its surrounding glory.

It was a similar experience with "Where the River Bends" a western starring James Stewart set in the mountains of Oregon but to me it was as familiar as the Dulas valley. This had bad men and good men, spectacular scenery, a big river, a love theme, renegade Indians and a happy ending. I also have this film on video and I enjoy it sometimes especially on a wet wintry Sunday afternoon. Byron and I would act out the scenes from the film except where James Stewart and Arthur Kennedy fight it out in the swirling river. I don't think that Byron or I could swim so we improvised instead with a kind of shoot out with imaginary guns. We would get off the bus and buy ourselves a packet of chips each finishing them off before we arrived back at our houses relishing the little bits of batter left at the vinegary bottom of the packet.

Aunty Enid and my grandmother were excellent cooks but Aunty Enid seemed to be always working, bustling and scurrying around the house a human dynamo at top speed. One day two of my cousins had paid us a visit and we were all seated around the table watching nervously at my Grandfather who would give orders to all and sundry in a mock gruff voice, his hands black from working at his trade. Aunty Enid had cooked a beautiful dish of rice pudding which had just come out of the oven and was very hot. "Eat around the edge now, it's very, very hot. Remember" she said emphatically. My grandfather growled in his appreciation.

"Do you hear? Eat around the edge."

When the food was served my grandfather immediately attacked the rice pudding with a huge spoon, digging straight into the centre of the bowl and then exploded with indignation spluttering and swearing at the table. My two female cousins and myself could hardly suppress our laughter. Eiri and Menna turned a pink colour which gradually became purple and had to leave the table leaving the pudding to be finished by no other than myself. I still think to this day that my Grandfather knew exactly what was going on and was merely pretending to be both aggressive and stupid for in fact he was neither...but, at the same time, we weren't quite sure.

My favourite uncle would call to help around the house bringing with him a bag of potatoes from his garden. This was my inimitable boxing poet Uncle Gwilym. Short stocky and pugnacious but with a ready laugh he would fill the room with his good nature. He would pretend to box with me and mugging away bobbing and weaving collapse on the floor for a mock knockout. He would then utter the sweetest of poetic lines that he had written a little earlier. He had the knack of being able to compose almost on the spot on any given title. I was of course naturally impressed and proud. He would always make a comment on the length of my hair and said that I needed a good crop.

"Healthier boy..short like mine..good for you" and then so as to ensure that no malice was intended would come out with a joke or two that would have us all laughing. He would regale me with yarns about the great boxers he had seen or wished he had seen. Peerless Jim Driscoll, Jimmy Wilde, Freddie Welsh, Tommy Farr, Jack Peterson, Cliff Curvis and Ronnie James all of whom of course were Welsh. He'd top this story with the tale of him having a go at a local fairground Boxing booth.

"I was having a good go, like, left jab and all that, then in the clinch the boxer said 'I'm not going to hurt you mun. Calm down' and then when I relaxed he caught me one right in the guts and down I went but I got up and went the three rounds and got the money." Apparently my uncle offered the money to his mother who refused it when she learned that he had earned it in the boxing ring. She would have nothing to do with it and to her, in her sweet, innocuous way, boxing was as immoral as alcohol or murder. On top of that My Uncle's sitting room is full of books and he led the chapel singing from the front seat with a smile like an open book.

One day in the holidays, after having enjoyed a lovely mid day meal, Grandfather sat by the fire smoking his pipe and occasionally spitting into the fire making it sizzle and I was reading from my Robin Hood book when I looked up to see, to my utter horror, a large black snake come slithering under the front door. For a second I thought I was dreaming and this was a poisonous reptile which would kill us all. I cried out to my Aunty Enid who came immediately and at her shout, my grandfather jumped up and in a flash strode out to the back kitchen, picked up a shovel or a spade and removed the horrific intruder. I stood transfixed in cold hypnosis as he manoeuvred the unwanted guest out the front door. Later the harmless but very dead grass snake lay hanging on the gate much to the surprise and disbelief of any onlooker. Little fuss was made of the episode but I still shudder at the memory and what if I had not spotted it and then come across it in my bed.

I had stayed with my other Aunt at a small holding on a hill overlooking the village. My aunty Megan and Uncle Gweirydd who was a collier by day and a smallholder by night, had no children but she was very fond of me and was kind although she did not spoil me. My Uncle had a large carton of Woodbine cigarettes under the settle but, although it had crossed my mind, I did not steal any of them. However Keith Lewis, a lad of similar age and mischief who lived nearby introduced me to smoking. It was a packet of Kensitas with a picture of a man in a dinner jacket on the front. He either was the waiter serving a drink or some Toff enjoying himself. They were cork tipped fags and I enjoyed trying them out in the ferns above the house. I don't know or did not ask him where they came from but it was good fun to be so naughty. He also tried to initiate me into the strange and troubled world of female sexuality but I was too canny for that. But only just!

When my father came to collect me at the end of the week I had a little present for him which was a comb in its own little sheath almost like a dagger and for my mother a box of chocolates bought at "Siop Salli". I think I gave my sister a packet of Rowntrees fruit gums and a crunchie bar to my brother. It had never crossed my mind to have bought something for my Aunt Enid who had cooked all the lovely meals or my ageing grandparents. As they say, eaten bread is soon forgotten.

And as for the FA cup final that year. If someone had scripted it as a film story they would have been ridiculed for being too far fetched and outrageous. I remember it being a fine day as I was winning my own match with Dennis 16-13 half listening to the commentary coming from the radio in the kitchen. My mother had sensibly opened the window and we would scamper over to hear the score every now and again. When Bolton was leading 3-1 I thought it was all over for the great Stanley when suddenly my mother shouted that Blackpool had scored. My personal game was abandoned immediately so that we could hear the final moments of the now famous match. Then Blackpool drew level and we started to bite our nails as the tension grew. In the last few minutes Blackpool went ahead through a goal from Perry and Blackpool had won 4-3. I felt sorry for Bolton and Nat Lofthouse as they should have won being so far ahead but really delighted that Stan Matthews had finally attained his winner's medal. Typically, in later years when interviewed, Matthews would willingly concede that it should have been Stan Mortenson's final as he had scored a hat -trick. It was the grace and modesty of the great man that made him such a hero in the eyes of the public. Today, if pushed. I can still name the whole of that cup winning team from George Farm in goal to Bill Perry on the left wing.

When I went back to Beulah school in September of that year I knew that big changes were on the way as I would be starting Builth School in twelve months' time and be among the big boys and everything else that was associated with that. I was growing in stature, starting to inherit the square miner's shoulders of my maternal grandfather but I was not prepared for the bigger changes that were to take place in my life. These changes were waiting like lonely horsemen on the far horizons; changes that were beyond my control.

****

Chapter Eleven
Builth School

There had been no serious preparation made for my starting at Builth School and I seem to recall merely going through the process without any serious mishap. There were others from my primary school also entering a new world so I was far from alone and I think we all just drifted on the slow tide that took us into the harbour of Builth County Secondary School. I felt secure knowing that my best friend in Beulah, Derek, was going to be with me and sharing the same feelings or emotions. I was a little reluctant to leave Beulah school where I had been so happy and contented in the company of Mr Davies and Miss Morgan for other than a brief time at Hendy, this was the only school I could really remember and a place that had laid the foundations and set standards for me.

My brother, of course, had been at Builth for a couple of years but he was no help, regaling me with horror stories of younger boys being ducked in the toilets, or beaten up behind the sheds and so forth. He did not try to make it any easier for me. There was even a whiff of envy from me when I received my school satchel which looked cheap and was I think imitation leather for Gareth had been awarded a beautiful real dark leather bag which turned a lovely deep red colour after a few months. He had also received a bicycle for passing into the County. Was I to receive a similar gift? I had already starting wearing grey flannel trousers which naturally were a little too big for me and I remember seeing my reflection in the window of Tyisaf when I walked to chapel one Sunday morning. I sensed that I was becoming a young man. Well physically anyway. Now I had my brand new blazer from Watts the Clothiers where Mr Mendel Meredith treated each customer like visiting royalty, and a red and green school cap which I hated, a white shirt and a striped tie. There was a geometry set, a ruler, a rubber a selection of pencils and my mother loaned me her old fountain pen which leaked a little and was a pale blue colour.

The morning beckoned without any trepidation and soon I was kitted out, scrubbed and standing at the crossing along with my brother and one or two others to await the school bus. I was excited at the thought of a new school and hoped I'd be able to get into the school soccer and cricket teams as well as defending myself ably against what bullies I might be confronted with. How would the teachers react? Was the cane still in use? Did they really duck the new boys? I did not like the water very much and I had never learned to swim. The green bus came at last trundling down the pitch to stop at the crossing. The engine ticked over noisily as the door opened. Derek was in the front seat looking like a choir boy, hair greased and combed and had kept a place for me which warmed my heart and increased my sense of confidence. The bus was full of red and green laughter and general silly banter. My brother retreated to the back area to join Mick Jones and Pearl Price amongst others. I recall seeing Pam sitting quietly in a passive sense of calm and this also pleased me but I wasn't quite sure why. The driver tossed his brylcreemed hair back and continued on the scenic route to Builth picking up children at various vantage points on the way. David, Tony and Glyn entered and paid little attention to Derek and I because we were the rookies but Tony grinned in a defeatist kind of way and ambled to an empty seat. I don't think he had a satchel or any possession other than his jacket.

When we arrived at the little town we encountered several other green buses parked rather haphazardly outside one of the chapels where the pupils were herded in to the interior for school assembly. I remember that on that particular morning I stayed with Derek and despite the hurly burly and the clamour of excitement, we eventually found ourselves in a classroom to sit what purported to be an entry examination. Everything appeared a shambles as instructions were given and we did our level best to follow them. There was an English test where I found the questions well within my comprehension and where I had the chance to write a composition involving a selection of items. This easily fired my imagination and I created an exciting yarn where the action continued at breakneck speed incorporating a robbery and using every cliché and revisiting every plot I had read in a comic book or seen on the silver screen. When I had finished I was quite tired but felt satisfied that I had done my best. There was a break and a dinner hour where we ate in a canteen somewhere near the road and then there was a test in Arithmetic which I barely managed to complete in the allocated time. I did not find it easy but coped with the problems. "If it takes a car three hours to complete a journey of fifty miles how long...?" One boy from Cilmeri was quite distressed at not knowing what the word "total" meant. I was on the point of telling him but thought better of it as I caught sight of the teacher at his desk looking over his glasses like some character out of Oliver Twist. My mother's pen left an inky spot on my forefinger and my head ached but the first day had soon come to an end and before I knew it I was scrambling back on the bus with its noise and general carousel and heading home to tea a change of clothes and the comfort of the kitchen.

The next day the same routine although on this day there was some singing from the rear of the bus led by the inimitable cheeky faced Mick Jones..... "There's a tiny house..." which we all joined in on the ridiculous chorus. The driver took no notice, tattooed and nicotine stained, a budding Teddy Boy, he merely smiled and studied his own reflection in the rear view mirror cigarette drooping nonchalantly from his lips. Derek had acquired a cheap mouth organ and could play a hymn tune on it. This was rather apposite to two intrepid travellers hoping to get into the county." Love divine all loves excelling....the happy pair were married.... ." and so it went on until we reached the town to be once more ushered into the swelling chapel by some fussy teachers, one of whom wore bicycle clips and shouted out instructions like an army officer. Today a sixth form boy in neat clothes played the Trumpet Voluntary on the pipe organ or it might have been "Jesu Joy of Man's Desire" before the Headmaster addressed the school. A list of names was read out and these pupils were to go to a certain room for registration. For some reason my name was called out first. To this day I do not know whether I had come top of the class or if the names had been drawn at random. They would hardly have been in alphabetical order. So I went along with Derek to class 2A where we were greeted by our Form Teacher Mr Richards. There was an air of expectancy and a foreign feeling within me of relief and satisfaction. The class looked like a bunch of refugees from the war with bulging cardigans and ill fitting blazers and trousers that were far too long in the leg. Added to this was the curious smell of daps and dogends, dubbined boots, chalk, urine, peppermints and bottled ink. I looked around the classroom and spotted Pam but not Tony. The rest were all strangers to me but not for long as we soon settled in to our new class and our new teacher. Mr Richards was a Pontypridd rugby playing man thin and with a long face and I think this may have been his first teaching post. He was serious but kindly and we felt at ease in his company. Even though this event happened a long time ago; September 1954, to this day I can recall the names of all the pupils that started that day in my class. I know there were many called Jones, a few named Williams and Price and a young dark haired lad ridiculously called Daniel Beebee who was quite naturally hailed as Bebee Daniels after the Radio star of that time. He did not stay very long, neither did a pretty girl called Karen Allen for whom old Schooly was willing to carry a torch!

We as a class soon got used to the daily routine and it was strange at first to travel from our base to other areas of the school. I had been used to a tiny village school where I knew everyone and now I was a grain of sand on a pebbly beach. Some of the older boys appeared as giants with shoulders as broad as a barn door. Others were pale and spotty who sniffed into their soiled handkerchiefs and blinked behind their glasses. The boys had to go down to the Strand to receive our Metal Work classes with Mr Gibbs whilst the girls did Needlework or Cookery, and also close by we had Biology lessons from Mr Reynolds who was very kind and very clear in his instructions. He was semi invalided and spent most of his time in a wheel chair. What fascinated me was his ability to write with either hand on the blackboard. The Metal Work classes were like brain surgery to me and all I recall of them now was trying desperately to solder two pieces of metal together with a shaking hand and placing Malcolm Jones's nose in the vice! Had I not learned anything from watching Jim Matthias in his smithy shoeing the horses and working the bellows? Similarly with Mr Scott in the Woodwork class, I managed to wear my apron correctly but could barely succeed at sharpening a pencil such was my dexterity or to be more precise, my clumsy inability to do anything practical. Mind you, I could have shown Mr Scott how to make a bow and an arrow or to gouge with a pen knife my initials in a tree. I had learned these skills from Mr Williams the Villa. My brother of course had made a beautiful wooden stool which had ornate carving as well as perfect joints and had its pride of place near the fireplace in the front room.

I was happy to do English with Mr Corfield although I had reservations about his sense of humour and enjoyed reading as a class Robert Louis Stevenson's Treasure Island. I especially liked Blind Pew who had scared and thrilled me when I had heard a version of the story on the radio as he tap- tapped his way to the Tavern. There were one or two slow readers in the class and I remember a farm boy mispronouncing the word champagne calling it "shampagnay" to the utter amusement of the others. I was also disturbed by the fact that John Payne, a character straight out of Fagin's den, would fall asleep during the lesson despite the obvious excitement of the story. He sat alone most of the time and did not have a blazer, wearing an old grey jersey that was too small for him and he always looked cold and undernourished.

In looking back at those innocent days, Builth County Secondary School was in a sense, a truly comprehensive school although the word had not been used then in educational senses. There were three streams: A B and C. Those in the A stream followed a more academic course and those in B would follow a simpler version whilst those in C were taught the basics and were more or less allowed to get on with it. Boys from 2C would be seen doing gardening or cleaning the buildings happy and innocent. We all joined forces for sport and the football matches that were arranged became quite a battleground where the frustrations of not being able to meet certain academic requirements were let loose with flying boots and sharp elbows. Often the soccer field was littered with sheep shit so the sliding tackle became more significant and powerful. There was a handsome fair haired boy called Jimmy Graham who excelled at football, smoked cigarettes behind the sheds and was very popular with the girls. Tony also showed his footballing prowess on the field and I was glad to have his company for a while playing along side him. I preferred to play at outside right, Stanley Matthews's position and Tony would play inside right taking my through ball pass and going at it like a demented greyhound. You had to watch out for your legs when tackled by someone like "Boko" who lunged at you and hoped to bring you down in a snorting, laughing, untidy tangle. Of course there were no showers after the game and you remained in class with dried dirt on your knees and nursing the inevitable bruises. Derek on the other hand was growing to become a sturdy lad and was picked for the school team even though he was only in the first year. I was very proud of him and bore very little resentment or envy.

We all settled in and apart from a few skirmishes everyone got on with the business of survival and learning. Break time was spent either drinking milk which I hated and soon abandoned or eating delicious Wagon Wheels purchased from Jane's Parlour on the Groe. It was the traditional Tuck Shop and we queued up patiently for our crisps and chocolate bars and the like. The Wagon Wheels were delicious chocolate biscuits packed in a light tinselled packet. Here we could safely sit and chew whilst on the swings or the various park seats. There was an idyllic background with the rows of Horse Chestnuts in full dying colour and the beautiful Wye flowing on its way to England. Here the older boys would hone their heading skills with a tennis ball and I longed to be a member of the party as they discussed tactics for a forthcoming match and how they were to approach the game. I recall someone called "Daisy" who was a very accomplished Goalkeeper and I am told went on to represent his country at schoolboy level.

One day early in the term I was chewing away and talking to Pam and Hazel Edwards on the swings when one boy in our class for no reason other than he felt like it, swung two punches into my face and then clattered off leaving me with a singing left ear and a swelling cheek. I refused to run after him but I was hurt and bewildered and embarrassed in front of my two female friends. In all fairness the girls pretended not to have noticed anything although my face was burning. I longed for revenge but I knew that fighting would get me into serious trouble and I would probably get hurt as well in the process. Soon afterwards the boys were lining up outside the Church Hall for our PT lessons led by Mr Wilson, when the trainee bully attempted the same tactics with Derek. In a flash of inspiration Derek threw three or four straight right jabs into the boy's face and followed up with a couple of left hooks to finish the job. The bully grinned sheepishly and with a red face scampered into a corner like a beaten dog. My heart raced, for revenge was sweet and there was no more trouble from the boy after that. It is interesting to note that the culprit who had so troubled me went on to become a Policeman in the Mid Wales Force!

We did History with Mr Bicknell who seldom smiled and was a miserable and sarcastic teacher who was unkind to some of the country girls trying to make them appear stupid and foolish; Physics with Mr Baynham where I dreamed of everything else besides the subject, teased the girls by pulling their hair or undoing their ribbons and was a pain in the proverbial. I had no interest in the subject at all. I seem to remember some simple experiment he made: the heating of a metal ball which would not go through a hole because of expanding and that Irene Price was very pretty, Ann Like was very tiny, and would I play for Pritchard house in football and would Jet Morgan be safe in his new space ship? Miriam Price was a dab hand at the subject and perhaps she had let me copy her work? Mr Nicholas took us in RI and he was a kind and serious academic who taught Latin to older students. I enjoyed his lessons immensely and after all, my father was a Minister of Religion and I told Mr Nicholas that very early on to establish myself so to speak! I remember that he smiled and nodded sagely as if I were a member of a troupe of visiting evangelists. In those early days I wasn't too sure if the young man who was the school secretary was in fact Dirk Bogarde or had I seen Bryngwyn Griffiths in Appointment in London screened one Saturday night in the Castle cinema?

I cannot for the life of me, remember studying Chemistry or indeed if there was such a thing as a Chemistry Lab. It's a compete blank. There was no Drama then as a subject, no Dance and very little Art. There was a school production of She Stoops to Conquer which I did not see but we were given a sample of it one afternoon. This may have been a dress rehearsal or merely a publicity exercise but I know that I could not have gone to see it in the evening. I have a vivid memory of Gloria Conti dressed in a very attractive costume that gave enticing glimpses of her cleavage and Jeff Jones hamming away as if his life depended on it. I think it was Michael Lewis's older brother that showed off as Tony Lumpkin shouting and stammering pretending to be drunk. I was enthralled and longed to join them in their scenario. I recall a school concert in the Strand Hall where my brother sang a comic duet with a girl from Llanwrtyd "Oh soldier, soldier won't you marry me with your musket fife and drum...? "The boys loved it, whistling and jeering and my brother hated it. But in all fairness he was rather good although I teased him about it and then immediately ran for cover.

One other day in school we were entertained by a visiting trio of musicians that played chamber music in one of the larger classrooms. They were named the Dorian trio comprising three old fashioned ladies in long grey dresses, pinned hair, glasses and beads, one of whom played the cello whilst the others played a violin or viola. I have no idea what they performed on that day but it was very thrilling to hear live resonant music from these three eccentric characters that bowed and smiled as we clapped. It was a nice change to be excused lessons and we sat dutifully and applauded with great gusto even though the content was largely way over our heads.

We had languages but I opted to do Welsh rather than French and had a very comfortable lesson with Miss A.S.Jones in the company of my two native speaking friends: Colwyn Jones and Miriam Price. We were treated as special and we had a few laughs and did some real work. Sally Jones as she was known, was smashing and like an Aunt to us sharing the language intimacy that the other class mates could not and treating us as favourites much to the contempt of some others. I think she gave us peppermint sweets as well but that might be stretching my imagination a little too far. Later on in life, I believe that she married Mr Bicknell of all people who certainly did not speak Welsh, and went to live in Garth.

The highlight of the working week, other than PT and Games, was the Music lesson with Mr Rogers. Mr R.S. Rogers was a Welsh speaking dapper man originally from North Wales with a short hair cut and a tuft of grey hair that stuck up at the front reminiscent of the boy hero in Tin Tin. He was a highly educated man, taught French at A level, very kind and had a wonderful individual approach to music. He did not worry too much about discipline and would occasionally shout. "Don't talk!" which in general was ignored by all and sundry. There was no allocation of desks so we sat or stood wherever we liked and naturally I spent my time in the company of the girls and got up to my usual tricks and nonsense. There was a small music room which had an old upright piano the keys of which were heavily pockmarked and stained. Mr Rogers would pound the chords on the piano and we would all attempt a choral rendition of such pieces as "Water Parted from the Sea" and " Hark Hark the Lark", In our childish moments of playful glee we would substitute the word "farted" for "parted" and considered this act of incursion very original and funny. Mr Rogers was known by all as "Barney" and seemed to enjoy his musical adventures with the misguided and maladjusted pupils under his supervision. We had a lot of fun and there was no malice in our endeavours only mischief and we really liked Mr Rogers and deep down we had much respect for him. However I must confess to being quite naughty and I never did get to find out the identity of "Who is Sylvia?....and what is she?" I dread to think what kind of a woman she was!

The days followed into weeks the trees on the Groe lost their leaves and the November fair, with its gaudiness and vulgarity came again and went again. We searched for conkers and the spent rockets from the bonfire night and received a rocket of another kind when late back to registration. We were allowed to go into the town at dinner time but I had very little money so other than on a Monday when the market was at full swing and the streets were crowded I did not bother much. Every Monday morning my mother would give me a shilling as pocket money and the first thing I would do was to buy my sister a comic. I chose Topper as it had cartoons in it and was colourful and very suitable for my young sister. The change, such as it was, would have to last for the rest of the week and I would eke it out as long as possible. I lost my cap so I promptly borrowed someone else's and then I lost my white penknife and I was quite upset about this. An older boy found it but would not return it to its rightful owner until a price of a tanner was proffered. I paid up and went on a diet for the rest of the week. The swing bridge over the Wye at the point where the Irfon joined it was out of bounds so quite naturally I went to have a look at it one day crossed it like a visiting colonist and despite the shaky construction managed to escape serious harm and avoided getting a soaking.

I did not always get away with things. Some of the older teachers had a rigid sense of discipline and used their hands to slap you across the head or cuff you behind the ear. One day I was running down the corridor and bumped quite unceremoniously into a teacher who was stepping out of the smoke filled staff room. I must have butted him in the solar plexus because he suddenly shouted at me and belted me around the head with his hands. If Mr Reynolds was ambidextrous in his ability to write on the blackboard this teacher was similar in his ability to smack my head with either hand. It was impossible to tell him that my attempts at GBH were purely accidental. Similarly one day whilst lining up for a lesson when I merely asked a question of Derek to be clouted very hard at the back of my head by a Mr Whiteman. I saw stars and nearly passed out from the blow. I detested the man from then on and mercifully he never taught me. I guess that was how it was in those days. The Headmaster was unforgiving too. This was Mr. PG Davies who I am told went up to Oxford at sixteen, ruled with a rod of iron and gave me an impression of Rocky Marciano in his study one fine day. He laid in to me with about four solid clips around the ears for having written something impolite on a desk. It was something along the lines of "John Samuels is a silly idiot ".I deserved to be reprimanded, told off and punished but to be half killed was unforgivable as far as I was concerned. Mr Davies was known as "Pig" by the pupils at school. I would have accepted the cane without a question as I had undoubtedly behaved in an inappropriate manner but physical assault was something else. However I did not mention it to anyone at home and let it pass.

Further disappointment awaited me. A boy in the class who lived in the town came up with a wonderful idea of arranging a football match on a Saturday between the town boys and the country lads to be played on the school field or the town's football pitch which was adjacent to the school pitch. I do not know how serious the game was to be but Tony and I were excited at the thought of playing in a real match and I soon made the necessary preparations of cleaning my boots, dubbining them and laying out my kit that had been washed and ironed by my mother. I even asked for a towel so I could have a quick wash afterwards. I begged my father to come and watch me play and although he had little interest in sport finally agreed to transport myself and Tony in the old car down to Builth for the morning's match. Of course when we arrived there, there was no trace of anyone else other than the boy who had thought up the idea. I was nearly crying with disappointment and was ashamed of myself for having dragged my father away from his work and for wasting his petrol and time. I never did find out whether the match had been arranged or was it just a figment of a stupid schoolboy's imagination. There was a feeble attempt at an excuse but it was my first experience of taking someone at their word and finding out to my dismay that it meant nothing.

Added to this was the misery of having lost my mother's fountain pen and this upset her almost as much as it had upset me.

Whatever the highlights of the week were, whether howling in the Music room or kicking hell out of each other on the football field, the lowlight was the Maths lessons and I hated these. I had always had reservations about my ability to understand concepts and many a penny wouldn't drop as far as I was concerned and then after having managed to master the technicalities of Long Divisions here I was confronted with two new enemies where there was no sense of reason and no understanding. I am talking of Algebra and Geometry which might as well have been taught in a foreign language as far as I was concerned. We had a young teacher who was nasty, had a strange accent and had no idea how to communicate with young people. He would speak with an unidentifiable twang, had a wispy moustache and leered at the girls. He was ugly and detested by all and sundry. He had a very disconcerting habit of creeping up behind you and twisting your cropped hair near your ear pinching it so hard that the pain was sharp as your face reddened. On other occasions he would slap you across the back of your head when you were bent over the exercise book. He also had a tendency to look down the front of a girl's blouse and once I saw him placing a ruler down one of the girl's front shaming her and embarrassing the whole class. We all knew of course that his manner and behaviour were out of order but we had little avenues of recourse and we just shut up and got on with it. Eventually I think somebody must

226

have reported him but by then the damage he had made on my mathematical career was beyond repair. "Let x be the unnamed teacher..." He moved on shortly afterwards whether to another post or to another career taking his dirty mac with him I hope. Good riddance to bad rubbish! I tried to get help with Algebra but it was beyond my father and of course my brother would lift his eyes heavenward and walk away from it all. I never did master the subject and now I don't care anymore!

Christmas came along with the exams and the school report which was favourable. I had done well in English coming top of the class, had excelled in R.I. and Welsh, good in History and Geography but indifferent in Physics and as far as Maths was concerned I was a lost cause. I remember vividly having to read the results of my exams. I had 29% in Arithmetic, 17% in Geometry and in Algebra I was thirty first in class with a percentage score of 3%. I am proud to say that it was only Malcolm Jones who was worse than I and became bottom with 2%. Malcolm did not seem to mind and enjoyed his visits to the modern and his revisits to the county. Very little was said at home about my utter failure as far as maths was concerned, my conduct was satisfactory and I was ninth in the class, Derek was tenth! I was quite happy about it all and swore I would try harder in the areas where I had failed. I had a new pocket knife that Christmas to replace the white one I had lost, but which had been found, and I started the new term with two knives and the burning ambition to collect all the picture cards of famous sportsmen given away with the ABC chewing gum company and to stick them in the album which I had acquired. The illustrious names ranged from John Charles and Dai Dower, the pride of Wales, to unpronounceable Hungarian footballers and other obscure names. I spent all my spare pennies on the revolting pink chewing gum and the wheeling and dealing that went on under the desks, together with the illicit love letters exchanged made school life more tolerable.

"I'll swop you two Len Shakletons for Arthur Milton!"

"No. Got him. Swop you for Willie Watson..." and so it went on. I was quite ready to get back to the new term but did not realise then that this was to be my last term and that by March of 1955 I would leave Builth for pastures new. Despite my fall from grace in Maths I could hold my head high and wear my blazer with some pride.

****

Chapter Twelve
Springtime is Returning

Despite my having managed to get in to the county school, despite having taking my few faltering steps towards maturity, there was still ample time for a few adventures in the rolling prairies of my vast imagination and a few sorties into self indulgent mischief. I would share the odd cigarette with Dennis who had access to them via his older brothers and I still got away with high jinks despite the warning shots fired across my bows. But beneath the outward merriment and cheerful disposition I suspected that my long extended childhood would invariably and inevitably come to an end.

I still rode my imaginary pinto to the badlands of Penrhiwmoch on a Saturday and spent hours with David either helping out on the farm in my most impractical manner or kicking a ball around until we were both exhausted. We were still good friends although we both went our separate ways when in school. David was beginning to see things in straight lines and was beginning to compartmentalise his friends and his actions. His school friends were those in his class and he would never bother much with Tony and I who were a year younger than him. Glyn Morgan was his special friend for they had started primary school together and I was not included in that special relationship. I was his Saturday pal and I was content with that.

Tony, on the other hand was not at all bothered about Builth School and continued to get into scrapes and indulge in mischief. One day I was with him at his home playing some silly game when we both decided it was time for a cigarette. Neither of us had any money but we waited until his mother went to the well across the road for some water and then he dived into a drawer, pulled out his red tin money box and in a matter of seconds had secured a shining half crown enough with which to purchase twenty woodbine and a box of matches. A trip to Llanafan was next on the agenda. Two angelic looking boys left the house and casually sauntered up the road.

"Where are you going? Remember be back for tea."

"Going for a walk up the woods."

As soon as we were out of sight of the house and the smoke that drifted lazily from the chimney pot, we ran as fast as we could until we reached the shop at the village. We paused to regain our composure but all I could feel was the pounding of my heart.

"You go in the shop and I'll keep guard."

"What will I say?"

"Tell Mrs Richards that the fags are for Mrs Jones Tyisaf."

Tony grinned and clutching the coin in his hand lifted his head and strolled into the shop. I could not hear the ensuing conversation because of the gurgling stream that rushed past outside, in a hurry to reach the safety of the river. I felt a painful twinge of cocktailed guilt as we had not only taken the money without consent but now we were telling straight lies. I tried to look innocent as I kept a wary eye out. I could see Gwyneth Oakfield hanging up some washing and she smiled and waved. I waved back. I heard the ringing of the shop bell and Tony emerged. We raced up the road, past Martha's cottage and the humble abode of the Wilson family, legs flying until we had turned a corner. We lit up and as we spluttered and coughed we laughed out loud and hid behind an oak tree as Artie Morgan caught sight of us. He grinned and said to me quietly.

"Does your father know, Preacher?"

I smiled uncertainly but he winked broadly and went about his business chuckling to himself.

"John Tyisaf smokes like this."

Tony inhaled showing his teeth at the same time and coughed violently so that his eyes watered and then he laughed uproariously rolling into the hedgerow, cigarette held high for the entire world to see. I stood there posturing like a matinee idol trying to pretend I was a gangster or cowboy bandit. By the end of the long afternoon we had managed, between us, to practically have completed the whole packet sitting amongst the green ferns by the rocks of the Hidden Canyon where only sheep showed the slightest of interest in our smoky world of make believe.

I had to go with David, one day, to Pencaeneuadd to collect some bread that had been left there by Downes's van. I suppose that Mrs Davies the Rhiw was away for some reason. She might have been visiting a sister ill in hospital so the bread, usually collected at the Rhiw was this time to be retrieved from the small holding about three hundred yards away. Pencaeneaudd, like the Rhiw had a roof that sloped down to the hill under which it stood so it was as easy as pie to clamber on the roof, yet again, for some mischief. I could not resist the temptation but David wasn't too keen but was easily swayed by my ambition to have a peep through their skylight. I led the way manoeuvring my way up the black slated roof which glistened in the pale sunshine of the afternoon. David waited on guard so to speak when suddenly the occupants, Gwladys Williams and her aged mother returned. I froze like some aspiring Father Christmas literally on the slippery slope for I was invading her home and she was in a temper. Serve me right!

"Get down from there now you naughty boy before I put this stick across you!"

I slithered and scurried down the incline of the roof and caught David's eye. His face was red and his eyes white. He had to collect the bread but much to my shame I made a bolt for it abandoning my friend. Gwladys stood there, her stick waving through the air as if she were landing a plane on the field, shouting in a frenzy of temper.

"You wait. I'll tell your mother about this and you'll get a good hiding. Preacher's son indeed. You ought to know better"

I trailed homewards whistling softly under my breath feeling a mixture of guilt, trepidation and a certain reckless sense of rebelliousness. As Gwladys was the local Post Woman who walked and tramped for miles on her round she would surely deliver the post to our house and would inform my mother of my innapropriate behaviour. Over the next day or so, I waited anxiously for my mother to admonish me but she certainly would not have given me a hiding that had been threatened. Nothing came of it and on the Sunday in chapel I wore the face of an angel but deliberately avoided Gwladys's eye. In all fairness Miss Gwladys Williams never told my mother about my indiscretion and once again, much to my relief I was reprieved.

A man called Ned Pryce came to lodge at the Rhiw. I think he came from somewhere near Machynlleth but he was known to all of us as The Moss Man. He was a rough diamond, dressed in a shabby dark trousers and waistcoat, an equally shapeless jacket that did not match the trousers, a grubby shirt, rolled up sleeves, no collar and tie and a dark flat cap. He had sinewy arms and nicotine stained fingers, dirty broken fingernails, yellow teeth and a gift for the gab. He told us that he was an ex footballer and had played as an amateur for Wales, telling us stories of games he had played in, promising Tony a football and once giving him a pair of old football stockings which turned out to be worn, ragged and like his stories I suspect, full of holes. His job was to pick and collect fresh moss from the neighbouring woods and fields and stuff it into a selection of large brown sacks later to be transported onto the back of an old pick up lorry he had. I presume the moss was eventually delivered to Covent Garden in London to be used in wreaths and bouquets and this is how The Moss Man made his living. He would leave the large and heavily bulging sacks at various points in the surrounding area and then collect them in one go so to speak sometimes using Noel Jones's gambo for this purpose. There was no road to the farm in those days. During our spare time we lads would help the Moss Man and once I received a six penny piece for my hard labour. On my way to visit David on a Saturday I would come across him sitting patiently near some trees, blue smoke emanating from his drooping cigarette, his hands clawing and picking as he crammed the strong smelling earthy moss into his sack as if he were a born again smuggler hiding his cache of stolen jewels. I wasn't afraid of him but there was nobody like him in the area and as a result he was of curious interest and a creature of fascination.

My parents on the other hand were a little more cautious and my mother was rather suspicious of this rough looking man. He called at our house once in his ancient lorry asking my father if he had any spare petrol. My father was persuaded by some means or other to siphon some petrol from Dad's car into the lorry so that Ned Pryce could be on his way. I remember seeing Ned produce a long piece of tubing where he paced one end into the car tank and then proceeded to suck some petrol until sufficient pressure allowed the transfer of the fuel into his own tank. It was clear that Mr Pryce had some experience in these matters but I don't think any money was exchanged between the two men and I stood fascinated as the Mossman drove away in a cloud of smoke and a crunching of gears. My father merely smiled as I once again asked the wrong questions to which no satisfactory answers were provided. My mother, on the other hand, shrugged her shoulders and turned her eyes to heaven.

I still visited the Williams family at the Villa and would often return home with a few silver coins, the remnants of a bristled kiss on my cheeks and my pockets full of mint imperials. They would speak to each other in English thinking that I could not understand them and we would play silly games like Hide and Seek which gave me access to the whole house. I thought nothing of entering their bedrooms hiding under the bed next to the chamber pot or retrieving a tin helmet from some cupboard or other. I would even open the drawers of Mr Williams's desk where he kept his private papers and his chequebook and it seemed the more audacious I became, the more the two old maids enjoyed it. The house was full of antique furniture and old china, priceless pieces that had been handed down over the years. One time David came to tea there and once again I was very naughty. At the table one of the sisters asked him if he liked tart and I replied on his behalf.

"Oh aye, Dai likes a tart now and again." This utterance caused him great embarrassment much to the blissful innocence of the two ladies. I recall his red face and rolling eyes and of course I loved every minute of it. Sometimes I would take my sister on my back crossing the little stream and entering the front of the house through an unlocked window and then picking up the rifle that Johnny kept by the door. I would burst into the room surprising them with the weapon in my hand. It does not bear thinking about now and I should have been severely reprimanded. Instead of which I was showered with affection and love. They were innocent and pure.

There was nobody like Tony. Who could run faster than he? He could climb trees, jump from great heights, clamber up roofs, ease his way through hedges and holes, dribble and shoot a ball of any size and accept any dare or challenge that came his way. He knew no danger.

"I bet you can't climb that tree."

"Oh yeh? Watch this then."

He would cling and swing like a monkey, hair down in his eyes, jersey hanging from his tiny frame, laughing and shouting as if there were no tomorrow.

One dismal day in early winter we were playing in the road outside my house when he had a notion of climbing the roof of the Blacksmith's shop across the road. Jim Matthias only worked part time now so we had ample time to embrace more mischief. I was reluctant as I had had my share of climbing roofs and was relieved that I had escaped from my previous adventure unscathed. I was not in a hurry to repeat it. The door was locked but Tony had this ridiculous idea of shinning up the drainpipe, scaling onto the roof and entering down the chimney. I resisted firmly as I could see the danger of one of us getting stuck in a flue and suffocating in the process. Tony was undeterred and began his ascent nimbly climbing the roof in a matter of minutes. I stood by watching helplessly on two minds whether to call my father and to bring this adventure to an immediate conclusion but I was compelled, enthralled by Tony's bravery or was it crass stupidity? He stood by the narrow chimney grinning inanely and began to shimmer into it. I began to cry out but my words froze in mid sentence as he suddenly slipped inside and disappeared from my sight. I looked around me conscious of the fact that might be witnessing the death of my best pal but I stood transfixed, helpless and staring at the skyline. Suddenly the door of the shop rattled, opened to reveal the chimney sweep urchin in the guise of Tony standing in the shadowed doorway teeth gleaming and eyes white.

"Come out now Tone." I breathed, pleased and relieved that my pal was uninjured and alive.

"Oh no. I have to lock the door and go back the way I come, otherwise they knows I been here."

At that, he closed the door and I heard the lock turning from the other side. I breathed heavily, apprehensive and suddenly grown up and fearful. I returned to the road, checking that my father was not in sight and waited for Tony to return. After what appeared to be an agonizing hour of trepidation, he suddenly re- emerged like a mole from the earth and in a matter of seconds scrambled and slid down the roof in an absolute state of filth. He trotted to the river bank and tried to wash off the majority of the coal dust and grime. He shivered and grinned and I was secretly pleased that I was the only one to have witnessed this act of daring. I did not realise then, but I was anachronistically reliving a scene from Dickensian times, the days of chimney sweeps and awful child labour. There was nobody like Tony.

Christmas came and went with the usual fun and games around the Christmas tree in the old school room, singing all the old favourite carols to the out of tuned piano as we waited for the ageless Santa and the windows steamed up as the fire in the grate burned with a fierce glow. Next on the social calendar's agenda was to enter the Eisteddfod. I do not know to this day who came up with the idea but somehow or other David and I, along with Glyn and his younger brother John were to compete for the quartet singing prize for competitors under fourteen. Mr. Davies the precentor at Troedrhiwdalar chapel agreed to coach us and we would meet him after Sunday school and one other day at Penrhiw getting off the school bus there on our way home. He was a quiet little man, kindly and very patient and he coached us with a warm understanding. I don't remember a piano at the house but I suppose there must have been unless Mr Davies used a tuning fork. There were four voices each singing a harmony to the main tune. I doubt whether our voices had yet broken but we took it seriously enough and to my ears it sounded quite good.

"Springtime is returning, the winter cold and grey with snow and nipping frost will soon have passed away"

About a week before the eisteddfod Mr Davies, his brows concentrated and face twitching with excitement said.

"You sing like that boys and you'll win the prize."

I was looking forward to it as I enjoyed the thought of performing and basking in the glow of the audience not to mention the distinct possibility of earning a shilling or two in the process.

David and I after spending a day together on the farm were walking up past the farm buildings as the winter shadows were drawing in. He was sending me as they say and we had approached the gate on the edge of the Wenallt woods I clutching the butter in my hand. We were discussing the fortunes of Spurs and Blackpool when I espied a shadow of a figure emerging from the woods. It was an old woman short, squat wearing an old gabardine coat a pair of wellingtons and a old battered brown felt hat. All that appeared to be missing was a broomstick and she carried a selection of shopping backs the contents of which smelled. She was a local woman who often was seen walking the streets of Builth on a market day remonstrating to herself in a loud voice. She seemed not to notice us as we gaped at her in a shock of horror and genuine fear. She was mumbling and grumbling to nobody in particular accusing somebody or other of stealing plums from her garden. Suddenly she saw us and came walking towards us in a menacing manner still accusing someone of many a misdemeanour. We turned and ran blindly back to the buildings where David's father was locking up the animals for the night. Breathlessly we blurted out some story or other that we were to be massacred on the spot. Noel Jones stood tall and thin with a long stick in his hand, cool and unafraid whilst Dai and I stood a little distance behind him in awe as he confronted the poor eccentric old lady who carried her belongings with her. A bag lady of the nineteen fifties!

Gently but firmly Noel Jones directed her towards Tyncoed, which was only about four fields away and where Mr Protheroe, I believe a relative, would take control of the situation. I was to discover, years later that is where she wanted to go to stay the night in front of the fire in readiness for the market day on Monday in Builth. She was obviously confused and distressed but still ranted and raved about her nephew or cousins. By the time she vanished down the lane towards the nearby farm it was now very dark and I still had the journey home to face. I could hardly see more than a few yards in front of me but I had no option but to venture homewards without the aid of a flashlight or the rising moon. I was still quite frightened as a result of having met the bag lady in the middle of the woods and I bid a hasty goodnight to David and his father and began to pick my tentatively towards the jaws of the wood. David would be home by the fire before I reached the top of the hill and before I would descend through the thickly carpeted oak leaved pathway and then across another hill and through the broken ferns and crooked sharp stones and shale.

There was no moon that night and no Star of Bethlehem, only the blurred ribbon of the path suggesting that I was on the right road and indeed pointing the right way. I slithered on the damp, darkened leaves and looked up half expecting to see a Witch come flying by on a broomstick or a horde of screaming banshees as the leafless trees appeared like claws of a giant bird ready to devour me. I began to run now downwards into the mouth of the waiting abyss, heart racing and sweat breaking out on my broad forehead. Suddenly I stopped in a cold tangle of frozen confusion. On the path in front of me was a body lying across my way. What could I do? Had someone been murdered here tonight and was the killer still at large waiting behind the next oak tree to cut my throat in one foul swoop? I froze in fear and tried to accustom my eyes to the shape in front of me. Slowly I inched my way forward looking over my shoulder now and again to ensure I wasn't being stalked. The silence crackled around me as I approached the body and found it to be a bulging sack that the Moss Man had left behind waiting to be collected. I gasped with relief and made a foolish sound before kicking the leaves in disgust and galloping down the track without looking back, rolling and reeling I threw myself forward until at last the winking lamplight of Tyisaf emerged in the gloom like a lighthouse in a storm. I vaulted over the gate and now here I was on Terra Firma, the tarmac road that led to my house and my kitchen and my bed. When I got to the crossing and surveyed the scene, a faint glimmer of a pale moon emerged above the spiky tree tops and I could see the light in my father's study and the faint reflection on the grey river than ran past the door of the house. For a second or two it seemed that the world had stopped still, holding its breath, and I sensed once again that I was the only person alive on the earth and I was on the outside of a window looking inwards. It is a feeling that I have often experienced over the years; a sense of aloneness. The butter wrapped in grease proof paper had assumed a new identity, a different shape as my hand had gripped it so tightly. I opened the door of the house and let myself in to the warmth of the interior of my home safe and secure and I grinned at myself as I took off my coat and slipped off my shining wellingtons.

When my father told me, along with my sister and brother, that we were going to move away from the area, I was shaken, confused, upset and unhappy. My immediate reaction was that I had been a naughty boy, recalcitrant, rebellious and had almost set the chapel deacon's barn on fire, had smoked illicit cigarettes, sworn in the churchyard and had poked fun at someone or other and had failed miserably in Algebra. As a result my father, full of shame had been forced to seek alternative employment elsewhere and I would have to carry the guilt on my shoulders for the rest of my life. None of this of course was the reason for my father's decision. Nevertheless there had been no discussion about the move and this was a bolt from the blue. I was ordered not to say anything to anybody, not yet as it had not been confirmed. I could not entertain why we should abandon such a happy environment for the pagan landscapes of South Wales especially now as electricity had just been promised and a bathroom and toilet installed. The scaffolding erected outside the front door, which was to help the workmen install the necessary requirements but had also enabled me to climb up to the roof of the house to explore the chimney and retrieve a soft ball that had lodged itself in the troughing. For days I nursed the disappointment within me carrying it around tentatively like a wrapped parcel unable to share my feelings with my friends or to seek advice from someone else. Mother would laugh a little too loudly and make a joke of it all and this was always a sign that she was worried but in no way could she or my father sit down and discuss this as a family. That was how it was. This was how it was going to be and there was little I could do about it. In short I did not want to live anywhere else and a gloom came over me and a tiny spark within me, a spark of my own sense of spirit, went out never to be rekindled.

My father was a young, good minister who cared deeply for his flock and served his people well at all times. He was also a fine preacher with a resonant voice and a sincerity that reached out to embrace everyone. His voice at a graveside would offer real strength to those who grieved, offer a sense of stability to those who faltered, hope for those in sorrow and he was my father. He had been "called" by a chapel in Cwmbach, Aberdare in the Northern Cynon valley, who had obviously noted his potential, recognised his strengths and he had decided to accept the invitation to become their minister. Through his eyes it was a bigger parish, a predominantly Welsh speaking congregation, a nicer and more modern house, access to shops and public facilities, a bus stop outside the door, less expenditure on the car, and a grammar school for his three children. I came across the truth years later when reading through his papers that the main reason for his leaving Troedrhiwdalar was to enable his children to have a better education. Perhaps he was deluded.

My brother showed little interest in the move and was truly quite philosophical about it all and my sister was only a child and did not really comprehend what was going on. I, the middle child, had to take it flush on the chin. My childhood was abruptly coming to an end and I became quieter, more reflective, thoughtful and almost withdrawn as I tried to absorb everything that was going on all around me. My friends were real friends, ones I had grown up with and now I was to lose forever. I had settled well, was happy in my surroundings and doing well enough at school so that I would have a future of some worthiness. Now the Jericho of my security was about to crumble and come tumbling down without any warning and without any apparent reason. So it seemed to me then and so it seems to now a generation later.

So I started the Spring term in Builth school realising it was to be my last term there and my mother had quite shrewdly, with insight, given me an autograph book that Christmas which I now began to fill with the signatures of my school friends, some of my teachers and the chapel people whom I not only respected but loved and admired as well. Most of the scrawled names in my book are in ball point even the copperplate signatures of the Villa family and those of Mr Jones who had so valiantly tried to teach me in Sunday School and Mr. Protheroe superintendent of the school. Mr Alfred Jones had written something quite apposite in his beautiful black inked fountain pen. Various school chums had signed my book some with spider like indentations, others with a flourish. A few of my teachers gave their signatures and I even accepted Mr P.G. Davies's even though he had thumped me around the head. Both Tony and Dennis added theirs but for some unknown reason David's signature is conspicuously absent.

There was some compensation for my increasing sense of gloom. Each morning I had a wake up call not from an alarm clock, or the fiery cockerel from the field the other side of the river, or my mother calling from the kitchen below, but the sweet and high pitched voice of Bryn next door going off to work on his bike. I would creep to the window and watch with admiration as he stood by the little latch gate his bike at the ready and his packed lunch on his back waving goodbye to his infant son Jimmy safe in the arms of his mother Miriam.

"Ta ta darlin..ta ta......there's a good boy...". It was a statement of pure love and affection totally unselfconsciously uttered and I would witness it every working day morning and it filled my heart with joy and pride. A magical moment. As the gate shut and the latch clicked I would get up and prepare myself to set off for school.

I recall quite clearly the day I was allowed to tell my friends that I would be leaving. It was a Saturday and Tony and I were walking with David along one of the fields above the farm house. It was a field where we had played out our games of cricket and football. It was a cold day, frost still visible in parts of the wood where the February sun had not penetrated and where the blue smoke from the farm house chimney curled upwards in a straight line like a giant exclamation mark. My heart was racing as I plucked up the courage to tell my two friends.
"I've got summat to say...I have some news..."

We stopped by the gate and Tony sat on the top bar his spindly legs dangling in front of him. They both waited as I picked up a stick and flung it as far as I could watching it dip and fall until it disappeared into the broken bracken.
"We are moving away down to Aberdare..going in March.."
"Where's Aberdare?"
"Why are you going?"
Two questions asked in unison and what could I say? I tried to explain the reasons but I did not know the answers. Tony gave his little sad grin, a sign to me of once again being let down and David showed his solemn face and said very little. We trudged to the house and David told his

mother and when she looked at me she could sense the troubled feelings I had inside and said nothing for once and merely continued with her work.

The days passed slowly. The workmen came and finished putting in a new bathroom, took away the scaffolding and the house looked almost new. Little I cared. I began to withdraw deeper into my own private world where I was once a cowboy or pirate and now I was the condemned man. I began to worry about things, became undecided and uncertain not knowing where I was going and what new friends I would make. I became reluctant to talk to anyone about my move although, to be fair, Mr Richards in school was very positive and said that he knew the Headmaster of Aberdare Boys Grammar School and spoke very highly of him. Some of the farmers would tease me about leaving them behind and despite their attempts to soften the blow, and in their own way they did try, I found it hard to reconcile. I would walk over to David's farm most Saturdays wondering whether I would see the place again and in the privacy of my own little world shed many an anxious tear as I sang a song to myself to the audience of old oaks, one I had composed which sounded very similar to Sweet Violets but had my own words which gave me some crumbs and scraps of comfort.

I accompanied my father to Capel Rhos for his final service there and although the chapel was very tiny and smelt of damp and the old organ had lost its breath.

"There's something wrong with its belly..." the old lady with no teeth who cleaned the place had remarked, there was still a convivial atmosphere there. I do not remember the sermon but I am certain that the last hymn that was sung on that Sunday afternoon was "Jesus still lead on" and I remember with pride the last refrain being repeated as we sang in praise of the Lord. Very little was said as my father and I walked home afterwards for I was too aware of his own sense of leaving, knowing how happy he was among the people and how well respected he was. For the last service at Troedrhiwdalar I could see from the seat at the side where I sat with my mother, my father bending his head below the pulpit to confront and control his own cauldron of emotion, hidden from the swelling congregation, hidden from my mother who sat as impassively as a stone, but within my sight. It was a private moment.

We had a final practice the morning of the eisteddfod. All spruced up and hair wetted and parted we sang together in unison with Mr Davies confident that we had a good chance of winning the prize. Glyn was, as usual, unconcerned about it all and hated any kind of fuss. David was tense and nervous and kept licking his lips and grinning whilst John, the youngest of us just tried to do as he was told. I looked forward to it and wanted to win so that the people would remember me and be sorry that I was leaving. When we got to the chapel the down stairs was quite full, this being the afternoon session for the children and young adults. The serious business would be later. Our particular competition was somewhere near the end of the afternoon and we had to sit through all the children's activities before performing our piece. I don't remember the opposition, whether there was only one other competitor or two but we went up and sang with gusto and strict discipline.

"Springtime is returning......." Indeed it was, but for me it was the last spring and no matter how hard I tried I could not shake off the sense of loss I was feeling. I remember standing there with my singing pals proud to be a part of the whole scene, seeing the familiar loved faces, the gestures of support and encouragement and the look of pride when we of course won the prize. John, being the youngest of us was selected to go up to receive the award and the accompanying prize bags. I won a few shillings for my efforts. We went out and played in the churchyard pocketing our coveted coins and ate our sandwiches in the schoolroom enjoying the congratulations from our beaming onlookers.

I stayed for the evening sitting high in the gallery with my pals and I walked home alone afterwards in the early hours of the morning bathed in ghostly moonlight and the trees all white with frost. There was nothing but silence all around me; the buildings dark and unlit. Yet again, I was the only one left on the earth and the only sound to be heard was the crunch of my shoes on the frozen grass verges and the beating of my heart. I stood again at the crossing where the roads met and where each direction was clearly marked and to be certain I was still in Breconshire. I waited for a second or two in the still chilled air, hearing softly the tiny murmur of the river and in the distance I heard the call of an owl somewhere on the trail to a distant farm. I knew then that nothing would ever be quite the same again, that the happiness I had enjoyed, absorbed and experienced would never be so complete again and that standing at the crossroads had more significance and carried more irony than I could imagine then and that the drawing down of the blinds of childhood would soon begin and that the future was out of my hands, beyond my control and there was nothing I could do about it.

We spent days packing our belongings into tea chests and cardboard boxes. My father tied his books together wrapped in newspaper and string. My books I kept to one side along with my holster and pistol and my prized bow with the real arrows. Several people called shyly to pay their respects and to say their farewells. Some people could barely look into my father's face and others blinked back their tears and shook my father's hand.

"You come back to see us now..don't forget mustah Williams."

Miriam and Bryn were very subdued. They were about to lose their neighbours although it would be quieter now after I had stopped kicking the ball at the garage door. I had intended showing little Jimmy all the haunts of my childhood as he grew but this was now not to be. The men came early one morning in March with the big lorry and in a matter of hours the possessions were carefully stored in the back and all was shipshape and the voyage was about to start. The house looked forlorn stripped of its happiness and its cosy, intimate corners. As the lorry took off I climbed the stairs for the last time into my now bare bedroom. There were marks on the floor where my little bed had stood and holes in the walls where I had hung my guns with inscriptions in pencil written on the faded wallpaper describing the gun and its facility. Above the Wennallt the frost was rising and everything sparkled in the spring sunshine. The river smiled and sang but my heart ached. I sat in the back of the car on the passenger side with my brother who looked straight ahead and showed no emotion. My sister travelled in the front on my mother's lap while my father took the wheel. I don't recall anyone saying goodbye at the door but at the crossing stood the Villa family. John and his sisters Mary Ann and Catherine. They stood together like three old trees heads lowered body language speaking an alien tongue. I got out and embraced the two ladies and shook Johnny Villa's hand. I got back into the car and we drove off. I turned to look for one last time at the figures standing so disconsolately at the crossing and the old house, empty now except for the ghosts of a young boy's childhood. I could not stop the tears and I sobbed uncontrollably until the exhaustion of the effort prevailed. Nothing was said. Not a word of comfort was spoken, no warm hand upon my shoulder as my childhood came to an abrupt end that mid March morning.

****

Printed in the United Kingdom
by Lightning Source UK Ltd.
118082UK00001B/7-21